Freefare

Freefare

WELCOME TO THE AGE OF ENTITLEMENT

MARK A. KOVEL SR.

FREEFARE
WELCOME TO THE AGE OF ENTITLEMENT

iUniverse books may be ordered through booksellers or by contacting:

iUniverse
1663 Liberty Drive
Bloomington, IN 47403
www.iuniverse.com
1-800-Authors (1-800-288-4677)

ISBN: 978-1-4917-8674-1 (sc)
ISBN: 978-1-4917-8675-8 (e)

Library of Congress Control Number: 2016900425

Print information available on the last page.

iUniverse rev. date: 01/07/2016

Contents

PREFACE

I have been employed in the insurance industry for more than forty years. The greatest portion of my experience has been as an owner of an independent insurance agency. In addition to my agency management responsibilities, I served as the primary insurance advisor to our largest business clients. The risk management functions I performed for them provided significant insight into the management challenges they faced. I serviced a significant variety of businesses operating across a broad spectrum of commercial services. My observations combined with my own experience in owning and operating a midsize business led me to the conclusion that *owning and operating a small to midsize business is the most difficult job in America.* The business owner, in addition to being an expert in his or her field of endeavor, must also perform a raft of services generally performed within fully staffed departments in larger enterprises. Among them are human resources functions (including all labor compliance issues), financial management (including banking relationships, lines of credit negotiations, cash flow analysis), and risk management functions (including all insurance purchasing decisions, employee benefit design, retirement plan design, perpetuation planning). All of these functions carry with them a full array of federal and state compliance requirements.

One of my main interests outside the insurance industry has been the study of American history. I have always had a keen interest in the unique aspects of America's establishment and its development into the economic and political giant it is today. I have read hundreds of books and watched an extensive number of television specials that deal with the development of America. My passion dates back to my early high school years. I actually won an award in my senior year for my outstanding performance in American History (I read Arthur Schlesinger's *Coming of the New Deal* when I was a junior in high school). The majority of the books I have read over the past fifty years are biographies, history based, or historical-based fiction.

The combination of my passion for American history and my unique insight into the operational and compliance challenges faced by all American businesses brought me to a point of frustration. The ever-growing volume of federal and state regulations is destroying the small and midsize business environment. The escalating volume of tax levies is usurping nearly all the free cash that used to flow to expand businesses and create jobs. We teeter on the edge of a fiscal cliff, and little is being done to prevent it. How can we change direction without staging another American Revolution? I believe Freefare will be the first step on the path to the creation of a new American dream.

INTRODUCTION

Throughout the history of the world, leaders of every nation have been forced to find a way to manage the daunting task of controlling their constituencies if they intended to maintain absolute authority. Gaining support from those who participated in power and wealth was easy, but managing the majority of the populace deemed to be the have-nots was far more challenging.

Early political leaders established authority by building an effective military force and conquering surrounding lands. Once a strong leader successfully established dominion, they maintained control through repression and fear. Logically the leader with the most effective military force held the keys to the kingdom. Fearing for their lives, the majority of the population submitted to serve the leader. Slavery and serfdom became the traditional means of controlling those who were destined to support the kingdom with their labor.

As history moved forward, the concept of the *divine right of kings* emerged as the most effective method of perpetuating the kingdom's leadership. Established leaders of both church and state advanced the belief that members of the royal family were *divinely anointed* to lead God's people. Unwavering political loyalty to those divinely anointed royal families combined with absolute adherence to religious edict became the opiate that subdued the disenfranchised masses. Wealth was restricted to the royals and the church while the starving masses worked to serve God and king. Commoners, convinced by their religious leaders to meekly suffer through their worldly existence to achieve a glorified afterlife, rarely challenged the status quo. Pious loyalty to anointed leaders replaced repression and fear as the means to suppress any desire for change. Most occupying the lower rungs of the societal ladder meekly accepted their fate.

The outlook of the world's common class began to change with the discovery of the New World. After a century of colonization, a handful of freethinkers, an ocean away from the suppression of the royals, revolted and seized control of the American colonies. These creative revolutionaries immediately convened a continental congress and launched the world's only democracy. The enlightened leadership of this "American experiment" supported the newly formed democracy with the planet's first free-enterprise economy.

The yokes and shackles of the monarchal form of government were cast off, and a nation that offered opportunity to all became the shining beacon, guiding the way to freedom and self-determination. Suddenly dawn broke with the hope for a better life instilled in the hearts and minds of the suppressed working class.

America's unique combination of democracy and free enterprise created the framework to alter the flow of funds away from the royals and the church, redirecting significant portions of the global horde of wealth to the New World entrepreneur. The American experiment provided *everyone* with the means to achieve and earn. American capitalism initiated the first global steps along a path to a fairer method of wealth distribution. Commoners industrious enough to take advantage of America's free-enterprise opportunity quickly earned fortunes. For the first time in history, money began to move away from the great and powerful, flowing instead to those who grasped the fundamentals of capitalism. A rapidly expanding number of industrious working-class individuals realized that wealth could actually be created rather than inherited or forcefully seized. Capitalism flourished in an environment where family history and social status were no longer the prerequisite to achieving success. In the New World, hard work and ingenuity replaced family lineage as the means to achieve wealth.

The American free-enterprise experiment quickly spawned a new breed of man, the American capitalist. In a short time, a handful of these American capitalists emerged as the *best of breed* and began to dominate the global economy. Many who were formerly penniless immigrants began to accumulate massive fortunes while the European elite fought to maintain their status quo. How could the global elite wealthy class maintain their superiority when the general masses were allowed to take advantage of a free-enterprise economy to alter their economic condition? The American experiment opened Pandora's box, giving hope to the downtrodden everywhere. The free-enterprise freedoms gave hope to all classes of Americans. Everywhere else in the civilized world, political efforts to control the masses would be forced to transform if political leaders intended to maintain control.

It could be argued that the root cause of both World War I and II was the failure of established Old World governments to transform by providing economic opportunities similar to those in the New World. Millions of Europeans were suffering, and many were starving. The fall of the monarchies in Europe was an inevitable result of European royalty failing to properly acknowledge, provide for, and control their starving masses. The European elite's hoarding of capital, combined with their traditional propensity to openly flaunt their inherited wealth, brought the entire class to their inevitable demise. Firmly believing their armies would remain loyal and subdue any insurrection, these oblivious monarchs regaled in their daily lives, insensitive to the depth of universal suffering. Then, suddenly, things changed, and many of the European wealthy paid with their lives.

The collapse of the Austrian empire, the Russian revolution, and the rise of Fascism in Germany, Spain, and Italy were directly related to worker insurrection—the rise of the proletariat. The expanding middle class began to seek a meaningful way to capture their fair share of wealth and power. Frustrated and suppressed, this new middle class began to collectivize with the intention of forcing the political establishment to create a fairer means to distribute wealth.

Prior to the First World War, the Industrial Revolution had brought the working man only long hours and meager wages while the greedy business owners continued to selfishly retain the majority of profits. Old World business owners, like their political leadership, failed to acknowledge the gross inequities. The greed and apathy displayed by the elite wealthy class would eventually lead to insurrection.

Long-term political control demanded that global leadership find a way to satisfy the global masses who now believed they were entitled to the same economic opportunity enjoyed in America. The working man was essentially demanding a fairer means of wealth distribution. Piety, fear, and repression were no longer proving to be useful tools to maintain domestic tranquility. Political failure was inevitable unless a means to achieve the consent of the emerging enlightened population could be found. Every worker in the world was now expecting an opportunity to fairly peruse economic success. The poor and downtrodden were no longer merely hoping for better lives; they were demanding opportunities to meet their new expectations for better lives. They expected to receive fair compensation for their work and the opportunity to pursue a meaningful education.

The political tool that would become the primary vehicle to achieve the long sought-after goal of fair wealth distribution came to life in 1917. Woodrow Wilson instituted this new tool to raise the funds required to finance America's entry into World War I—the income tax. It quickly emerged as the global community's peaceful means to politically force an actual redistribution of wealth (as opposed to the opportunity to earn a fair share of wealth). Sadly, for those in need, the tax was instituted to finance the war effort rather than as a means to relieve the suffering of those unfortunate individuals who failed to grasp the concept of capitalism. Despite its use, Wilson successfully established what would soon become the universally accepted nonviolent means to limit inequitable wealth accumulation. This peaceful means to reallocate wealth had been successfully put in play to finance the war effort. After the war, even though the income tax was generally accepted by most Americans, Wilson failed to use it as a meaningful method to relieve the suffering of those who occupied the lower rungs of the economic ladder. That project would soon become the focus of the Franklin Roosevelt and Lyndon Johnson administrations.[1]

---

[1] Excerpts from *Woodrow Wilson*, The American Presidents Series, H.W. Brands, Times Books.

The chaos and destruction attributed to the two World Wars provided the catalyst for change. After the Second World War ended, Europe faced the daunting task of totally rebuilding. Every aspect of existence—political, industrial, agricultural, and social—faced reconstruction and would be altered for all time.

Russia emerged from this postwar era as the Soviet Union imposing the Marxist *Communist Manifesto* on every citizen from Eastern Europe to the Pacific Ocean.

In Europe, the economic condition of the lower class would no longer be ignored. Absolute monarchies would be replaced by socialist democracies that were pledged to institute a fairer distribution of wealth. Socialism was quickly embraced as the foundation on which a new Europe would reconstruct itself.

In America, FDR's New Deal, launched as an emergency measure to halt the Great Depression, became the transitional means to a socially responsible American federal government. Roosevelt's first hundred days in office forever altered the expectations Americans held for their national government. For the first time in history, the American president promised to take care of the common man. To achieve his goal, FDR fully embraced the power of the tax as an effective means to peacefully seize wealth, intending to redistribute most of the commandeered funds to those in need. FDR's initiatives became so warmly embraced that he became the only American president elected to office for four terms.[2] FDR's initiation of new social reforms served to illuminate the path to America's journey to the current age of entitlement.

---

[2]   Excerpts from *Nothing to Fear*, Adam Cohen, Penguin Press.

Following FDR's revolution, most world leaders began to embrace a new theory of political control that replaced *conquer and suppress with fear and religious piety* with a new theory: *gain power, pacify, then satisfy and control with social reforms and government dependency.*

The revised theory would bring social reform to the forefront as the primary political control mechanism. By the end of the twentieth century, all modern governments would adapt. Issues affecting the common man like medical care, retirement income, unemployment insurance, aid to the handicapped, and welfare for the unemployable would become key elements in the social reform/control agenda. These progressive reforms would establish the basis for the implementation of the updated theory of government (control with social reform and government dependency), altering the standard of living for entire civilized world.

Two decades after FDR, Lyndon Johnson would ascend to the US presidency, adding his own concept for social enhancements labeled "the Great Society." Funding existing programs like social security along with LBJ's new entitlements would quickly become a massive challenge. By the end of the twentieth century, the largest portion of the national budget was being spent on the key social enrichment programs: Medicare, Medicaid, and social security. The free-enterprise opportunity *to earn* fair wealth distribution began to evolve into a system of *politically forced* wealth redistribution, changing America from a country embracing entrepreneurial capitalism and rugged individualism into a country supporting entrepreneurial socialism.

In the course of two lifetimes, hope became the catalyst in the evolution of the attitude of the common man, evolving from meek acceptance into an expectation of opportunity, then quickly maturing into a belief that everyone is entitled to more than just opportunity. The majority of modern Americans now believe that everyone should be protected from economic depravity. Most believe the federal government, using funds raised through their taxing power, should provide a safety net for all people (citizens and noncitizens) on American soil. Once the common man embraced hope, the search for a better life created an expectation that could not be quelled. That expectation has now morphed into a sense of entitlement.

Today, federal funds dedicated to social programs and the vast bureaucracy to support these entitlements is expanding exponentially, yet many feel the actual support given to impoverished Americans is grossly inadequate. Despite the century-long focus on the needs of the disenfranchised, the economic gap between the well-to-do and those on the lower rungs of the economic scale continues to grow. This growing economic gap is eroding the American standard of living as the wealth of the nation is now being claimed by a smaller percentage of the population. Constant increases in tax levies and federal mandates (like the health insurance mandate) imposed upon wage earners have significantly eroded the average middle-class American's net disposable income. Stagnant wage levels and limited job growth have also served to suppress economic opportunity. Many who formerly enjoyed the economic comforts offered in the middle class are barely hanging on. The overstressed, overtaxed middle class continues to fall farther and farther behind the wealthy as the working American is now holding less spendable income than any other time in the past seventy-five years. Even the most conservative Americans recognize the potential threat this growing inequity represents.

The economic reality of capitalism dictates that wealth flows to those that create and innovate. Enormous amounts of money flow to those who drive the economy, the inventors, innovators, and those who create. The fundamental aspect of capitalism drives money to the winners; to the victor goes the spoil. Many of today's liberal social activists are advocating an interruption in this process of capitalism, promoting new concepts that will amend the tax codes to redistribute an even greater portion of the victor's spoil. Citing the enormous compensation paid to corporate executives, elite professional athletes, movie stars, authors, and Wall Street traders, liberal leaders feel it is unconscionable for a nation of such wealth to overlook so many impoverished citizens. No child should wake up hungry in a nation with such wealth.

Conservative economists believe any meaningful increase in the top-end tax percentage will destroy economic incentive for those who invest and create jobs (just read *Atlas Shrugged*). How then (baring a significant tax increase on the wealthy) can the economic gap between the haves and the have-nots be closed? Is it possible to devise a meaningful way to improve the financial situation of the underprivileged, impoverished American without destroying the economic foundation of the nation? How much money can be usurped from the winners without destroying the entrepreneurial spirit of those who create the jobs that drive the economy? Is there a method that can more effectively deploy the current tax revenue in order to develop a fairer means to redistribute America's wealth? Can America create a new updated version of itself by developing a system in which no one within our borders will suffer?

It is possible. Freefare is the answer.

PART 1

The Roots of Freefare

Chapter 1

The Free Enterprise Economy

The free-enterprise economic system, the principal cornerstone of American freedom, has been under attack for more than a century. We stand in the shadow of the most productive civilization ever created and wonder why it is crumbling around us, teetering on the edge of a fiscal cliff. America's economy, once the envy of the modern world, is poised to tumble over a financial ledge now that more citizens are collecting government benefits than paying taxes to support those benefits. The middle class is falling farther and farther behind in the race to economic independence, and a growing number are now facing financial disaster. The challenged middle class has united with the unfortunate in the lower class to create a political majority. Leveraging this newly established voting majority, they are demanding that all receive their fair share from the wealthy. The age of entitlement is at hand, and the American free-enterprise system is about to fade into history.

America's founding fathers fully understood that personal freedom is inextricably tied to economic freedom. One cannot exist without the other. The colonists fought the American Revolution to escape the onerous economic and political controls imposed by the British monarchy (think taxation without representation). These colonists, the new Americans, witnessed firsthand the impact that trade restrictions, taxes, and duties had on their ability to prosper. *Unrestricted economic opportunity* was the essential element in America's *freedom proposition*. The colonial Continental Congress was determined to create a political system that would eliminate all government interference with their newly established free-enterprise economy. The intent from the very beginning was to limit the size, scope, and power of the federal government. These inspired leaders established the planet's only democracy and then successfully restricted the economic authority of their new government, thus creating an entirely new form of government, the free-enterprise democracy. The founding fathers fully understood that if a political entity controlled the economy, it would also control the distribution of wealth, thus restricting the opportunity for success from those not in political favor.

The founding fathers' free-enterprise experiment established a social environment that offered unlimited opportunity to anyone who held a creative concept and was willing to put forth sufficient ambition to pursue a dream. The new democracy offered social and economic opportunity that existed nowhere else on the planet. The newly established American government imposed no general taxes, no sales taxes, no business regulation, no licensing requirements, and no restrictions on commerce.

For the first time in human history, man's mind, money, and ambition were set free. Fortunes were being created through hard work and ingenuity rather than through conquest and serfdom. The new Americans became the first civilization to use the phrase "to make money." No other language or nation ever used those words. Wealth had previously been thought of as a static quantity, limited in scale, that had to be seized, inherited, looted, or obtained as a favor. Americans were the first to understand that wealth could actually be created.

Immigrants flooded in to American ports from every corner of the planet. Millions left their ancestral home with little more than the hope in their hearts. They were seeking only the opportunity to reap the benefit of their own labors. No safety net, no food stamps, no welfare—just opportunity.

Honoring the founding fathers' initial concepts, the early Americans established two principal duties for the federal government: (1) protect Americans from foreign attack and (2) safeguard the personal and economic freedoms of the citizens.

From America's beginning, the main-street business was the center of the American free-enterprise economic universe. The opportunity to establish and run a business enterprise free from extensive governmental interference was the principal component of the economic promise conceived by our founding fathers. New World entrepreneurs capitalized on the lack of taxes and operational restrictions to establish businesses that they were free to run as they wished—a dream that could have never been realized in the Old World. American leadership fully understood that the wealth of the nation was dependent upon the citizen's ability to produce goods, the availability of manpower to produce those goods, and also the existence of a financially capable consumer willing and able to purchase what was produced. Any government interference with this economic model would serve as a dam restricting the flow of funds used to support the supply and demand for American products. The free flow of money circulating among the main-street business owners, their employees, and their suppliers was the fuel that fed the engine of American economic growth for more than a century.

Early American history is filled with examples of immigrants who seized America's free-enterprise economic opportunity. Many formed businesses that were small in scale—hardware stores, food and provisions stores, blacksmith shops, horse stables, carpenters, and other tradesmen. Thousands of small businesses formed to meet the primary needs of the local community. Most were able to generate a meaningful income. Nearly all were formed with limited capital, succeeding solely on the diligent efforts of the main-street businessman and the loyal patronage of neighbors. Unencumbered by governmental regulations, taxes, and controls, these courageous entrepreneurs were free to retain profits, reinvest revenues, and grow their enterprises to meet the escalating demands of new communities that were springing up everywhere. Most were family-owned businesses that prospered and were easily passed on to the next generation in an economic environment free from inheritance tax.

CHAPTER 2

The American Industrialist

America quickly became a country of reason, justice, freedom, production, and achievement. There were no fortunes by conquest, only fortunes by work. Instead of swordsmen and slaves, there appeared the real maker of wealth, the greatest worker, the highest type of human being—the self-made man, the American industrialist.[3]

By the start of the nineteenth century, the American economy was giving life to a surprising volume of these self-made millionaire industrialists. The typical industrialist would appear out of nowhere, build a business, and expand it to a point where the business controlled its related marketplace. A few of these enterprises were phenomenally successful, generating profits that were envied by their Old World competitors. Andrew Carnegie, John Rockefeller, and Henry Ford are outstanding examples of the typical American industrialist. All were determined entrepreneurs armed with productive business concepts. They were exceptional risk takers perfectly willing to put everything they had on the line. They bet all they owned and gave

---

[3]   From *Atlas Shrugged*, Ayn Rand, Penguin Books, page 440.

all they had. Their resulting success led to phenomenal wealth—created through hard work and innovation rather than through looting and conquest.

Andrew Carnegie, an immigrant from Scotland, arrived in the United States in May 1848 with his nearly penniless family. The family settled near Pittsburgh, Pennsylvania, where Andrew took a job in the boiler room of a thread factory, earning $1.20 per week. After a short stint in the boiler room, he was able to land a job as a telegraph messenger. That job led to a position with a Pennsylvania railroad. By the time he reached his eighteenth birthday, Andrew was preparing himself for promotion in the railroad. Within three years, he had worked his way up to a supervisory position. By the time he turned twenty-four, he was head of the western division of the railroad. At that time, using his mother's house as collateral, he was able to borrow $600 from his boss to invest in stocks. His resourceful investing soon created enough income that he was able to invest in companies that were developing sleeping cars for the railroad. These investments were the initial steps toward unimaginable wealth.

His business career took a turn in 1860 with the advent of the Civil War. He was selected to serve the Lincoln administration as a civilian advisor, serving primarily as a supervisor of telegraph services. With the successful conclusion of the war, Andrew left the railroad industry and began to focus on supervising his personal investments. Carnegie turned his investment focus to the steel industry. He formed Carnegie Steel and made it highly profitable through the application of the new Bessemer process. This innovative approach to making steel revolutionized the industry. Using this innovative new production process, he was able to grow his company into the largest steel company in the world by 1889. In forty-one years, Carnegie had gone from a penniless immigrant earning $1.20 per week to one of the world's wealthiest men. In 1901 after having experienced severe labor disputes, Carnegie sold his steel company to US Steel, reaping an extremely large personal fortune. Believing that a man should not leave his fortune solely to his children, he formed a philanthropic fund to which he donated $125 million. Most of the institutions supported by his Carnegie Foundation Fund are still in operation today.[4]

John D. Rockefeller was born in 1839 in Richford, New York. He moved to Cleveland, Ohio, with his parents in 1853. In 1855, at the age of sixteen, John took a job as an assistant bookkeeper earning less than four dollars per week. He soon set up his first business enterprise—a commission business dealing in hay, grain, meats, and other farm goods. In 1863, recognizing the opportunity stemming from oil production in Western Pennsylvania, John along with a few investors built an oil refinery outside Cleveland. The venture was successful, leading to the formation of Standard Oil Company (Ohio). Standard Oil then began acquiring other refineries in the Cleveland region. By 1882, Standard Oil had a near monopoly in the oil business and was generating millions in profit. In a span of just over twenty-five years, John D. Rockefeller had risen from an assistant bookkeeper earning less than four dollars a week to a multimillionaire. From 1882 on, John and his Standard Oil Company were constantly under attack by "trust busters" seeking to evoke the Sherman antitrust law to limit the scope of the company. John survived the attacks and grew Standard Oil into one of the world's most dominating businesses. After 1887, John began to turn his attention to philanthropy. In 1913, he funded the Rockefeller Foundation. Benefactions during

---

[4]   From History.com.

his lifetime totaled more than $500 million. The Rockefeller Foundation continues to exist today, funding many of our most familiar charities.[5]

Henry Ford was born in 1863 near Dearborn, Michigan. He was one of eight children of William and Mary Ford, who operated a family farm in Wayne County, eight miles west of Detroit. At age sixteen, Henry *walked* to Detroit to find work in its machine shops. After three years in Detroit, during which time he became familiar with the internal combustion engine, he returned to the family farm. He worked part-time for Westinghouse Engine Company and tinkered in his spare time in a little machine shop he had set up. Eventually he built a "farm locomotive," a tractor that used an old mowing machine for its chassis and a homemade steam engine for power. In 1889, he married Clara Bryant. Two years later, they moved back to Detroit where Henry was made chief engineer at the main Detroit Edison Company plant, with the responsibility of maintaining electric service in the city twenty-four hours a day. Because he worked no regular hours (he was on call twenty-four hours a day), Henry could experiment to his heart's content. Several years before, he had determined that he could build a gas-powered vehicle. His first working gasoline-powered engine was completed by the end of 1893. By 1896, he had completed his first "horseless carriage." Unlike many other automotive inventors, all of whom had built self-powered vehicles before Ford, Henry sold his operations to finance work on a second vehicle, then a third, and so on. During the next few years, Ford, with the backing of wealthy investors, continued to develop his dream vehicle. Eventually, Ford, after exasperating his investors by refusing to produce a

---

[5]   From History.com.

vehicle until it was ready for the public, was left on his own. In 1903, Ford determined that he was ready to market his new vehicle. The Ford Motor Company was incorporated with a mere $28,000 in cash, which had been put up primarily from the savings of ordinary citizens (in his previous dealings, Ford had antagonized the wealthiest men in Detroit). The company was a success from the beginning, but just five weeks after its incorporation, the Association of Licensed Automobile Manufactures threatened to put Ford out of business because Ford was not a licensed manufacturer (the association refused to issue him a license). Ford fought in court and finally won on appeal in 1911. The dream vehicle Ford developed was the Model T.

In the nineteen years of its existence, Ford sold 15 million Model T vehicles in the United States, another million in Canada, and 250,000 in Great Britain. The remarkable birth rate of the Model Ts was made possible by the most advanced production technology yet conceived. After much experimentation by Ford and his engineers, the system that evolved in 1913–14 in Ford's new plant in Highland Park, Michigan, was able to deliver parts, subassemblies, and assemblies with precise timing to a constantly moving assembly line.

Ford's subdivision of labor and the coordination of a multitude of operations produced huge gains in productivity. In 1914, Ford Motor Company announced that it would henceforth pay workers a minimum wage of five dollars per day (compared to an average of $2.34 for the industry) and would reduce the work day from nine hours to eight, thereby converting the factory to a three-shift day. The development of his new mass production techniques allowed Ford Motor to turn out a new Model T *every twenty-four seconds*. The Model T was the chief instrument of one of the greatest and most rapid changes in the lives of common people in history. In less than two decades, the automobile had become the main cog in the growth of the American economy and a major stimulant to urbanization. Ford died in 1947, exactly one hundred years after his father had left Ireland for Michigan. His holdings in Ford Motor Company went to the Ford Foundation, which had been set up in 1936 as a means of retaining family control of the firm. The Ford Foundation subsequently became the richest private foundation in the world. The foundation remains in existence, donating millions to charity every year.[6]

These new American industrialists did not come from money. They did not inherit their businesses. They did not have wealthy ancestors. They rose from the dirt, worked hard, took risks, and were devoted to success. They grew their fortunes unencumbered by onerous taxes, excessive regulations, and bureaucratic controls, building America by providing the products, jobs, and innovations that made the free-enterprise economy explode. Through the diligent efforts of the New World industrialists, America evolved into an economic giant that quickly surpassed the overtaxed, overcontrolled, overregulated economies of Europe.

Many liberal historians vilify these famous industrialists and many other business innovators for taking advantage of cheap labor, abundant raw materials, minimal governmental interference, and exploding demand. Should they be hated for suppressing workers' wages and manipulating the marketplace to achieve excessive profits? Or should they be revered for creating the jobs that fueled immigration and for developing products and application techniques that created the industrial revolution? These three and the many

---

6   From History.com.

other homegrown industrialists provided opportunity to the immigrants. The availability of jobs provided the paycheck that allowed these new Americans to house and feed their families. The work was hard, and often the pay was meager, but the jobs were the road to a better future. Without the opportunity to work, many would have been forced to return home. Each of the three industrialists cited here started with menial work at meager wages. They were able to seize the American opportunity to work and use that opportunity as a springboard to unfathomable wealth.

It should be noted that Carnegie, Rockefeller, and Ford each created well-funded charitable foundations from the wealth they created. These foundations have generously funded many meaningful American charities for more than a century. This begs the question, would America be a better country had the federal government interfered with the cost of labor and raw materials, thus usurping most of Carnegie, Rockefeller, and Ford's profits to fund welfare and entitlement programs along with the giant bureaucracy needed to support those programs? Had the federal bureaucracy successfully seized sizable portions of their profits, would these generous industrialists still have exhibited the generosity to form their foundations? Once looted by a punitive tax code, the profits likely would have been allocated to a massive federal bureaucracy, operating with giant budgets that earmarked future profits to fund assistance programs even before those profits were earned. Federal interference with the pricing and supply of raw materials paired with a mandated minimum wage would have limited growth, job creation, and product innovation.

Business regulations may have improved the situation for those workers who could find work, but fundamental business economics would indicate that the reduced cash flow caused by government taxation would have limited the available jobs. Any significant tax on corporate profits would have restricted the capital these rapidly expanding companies needed to grow and innovate. Fewer jobs and slower growth likely would have combined to limit the American dream.

America successfully navigated its first full century of existence without any federal income tax, without an estate tax, without a federal welfare system, without any significant foreign aid payments, without farm subsidies, without social security, and without Medicaid and Medicare. Everyone in America had the opportunity to earn a living wage and the freedom to keep what they earned. Most workers paid no tax; they were not forced to contribute to social security or to health insurance plans. If they earned a dollar an hour and worked a forty-hour week, they brought home forty dollars. Their paychecks contained no federal- or state-mandated deductions. During this era, Americans depended upon family, friends, and the generosity of their churches and local communities when times were difficult. No one believed they were entitled to any benefits from the state or federal government. Immigrants came to America for the opportunity to work and get ahead, not for the welfare, or a free education, or free medical coverage. They came for the opportunity to work and earn.

CHAPTER 3

The Rise of the Proletariat

By the late 1800s, the world began to change. Most foreign workers viewed America as a worker's utopia, as the model for economic and personal freedom. Hoping to emulate America's economic freedom proposition, oppressed workers throughout the industrial world began to collectivize. They organized into trade unions, and political parties formed to help extract the working man's *rightful due* from the wealthy industrialists.

Shortly after the turn of the twentieth century, the Russian revolution and the later rise of the Nazi Party in Germany offered graphic proof of the power of the collective: the world began to witness the rise of the proletariat. The working class began to establish a political foothold, and socioeconomic change was forced upon the unyielding wealthy class. The collectivization concept instituted to support the power of the working class was easily imported to America through the constant flow of immigrants.

By the start of the twentieth century, the steady flow of these enlightened proletariat immigrants began to effect a change in America's attitudes. The totally free-enterprise entrepreneurial opportunity so fully embraced by the early immigrants began to take a significant turn toward extinction when the imported Progressive Workers Movement began to take hold in America. Elected officials, following what they believed to be a higher moral code, began to pass legislation intended to control the business environment, protecting the common man from the American industrialists and the growing number of business monopolies (trusts).

By the start of the second decade of the twentieth century, a new moral code inspired by the Progressive Workers Movement became a force to be reckoned with. Leaders of the progressive revolution (union leaders and progressive politicians), seeking the political support of the proletariat, successfully amended the definition of the federal government's primary duties. The newly formed expectations were amended to (1) protect the citizens from foreign attack and (2) safeguard personal and economic freedom by creating a meaningful process to properly distribute wealth.

America responded to the Progressive Workers Movement and the new expectations of the federal role by electing its first progressive president, Woodrow Wilson. Using the unrest in Russia and Germany as a backdrop, Wilson promised substantial economic reform intended to aid the common man. He pledged his administration to battle industrial monopolies and greedy banks.

After winning the presidency, he seized upon his progressive mandate to develop the world's first peaceful application of the wealth redistribution theory, the income tax. Initially passed as a temporary measure to finance World War I, the income tax was enthusiastically supported by the majority of voters, as most were exempt from the initial tax. The new tax applied at an income level that affected only the wealthy. The resulting flow of tax revenue provided America's national politicians with their first taste of the tax and spend approach to federal government.

The newly instituted income tax, combined with other Wilson-initiated progressive programs, signaled the advent of radical social change in America. The establishment of a peaceful means to seize wealth for the benefit of the multitude illuminated the path to the current age of entitlement.

Wilson's term successfully planted the seeds of change that would soon bring us the FDR revolution. Pandora's box was open. America would never be the same, and the world was watching.

The election of Franklin Delano Roosevelt and his first one hundred days in office should be thought of as America's *second revolution*. His administration launched a three-month assault on the free-enterprise system during which FDR and his administrative cohorts successfully established the foundation for his New Deal. By the time he was done, most Americans began to believe that the federal bureaucracy should control and manage every challenge faced by the common man. The implementation of FDR's New Deal substantially altered the American psyche. The massive extent of federal assistance initiated during the FDR revolution brought America to the next level in its evolution—the conversion of the America free-enterprise system into the world's first functioning welfare state.

The next step in America's cultural/economic evolution began with a catastrophic event that occurred on November 23, 1963. John F. Kennedy, the youthful hope for America's future, was assassinated in Dallas, Texas. Kennedy's leadership inspired many new economic objectives. He understood that overdependence on government assistance had to change ("Ask not what your country can do for you;

ask what you can do for your country"). Change and hope died with Kennedy. Lyndon B. Johnson, another inspired progressive, ascended to the presidency. Using the sympathy surrounding the assassination of John Kennedy, Johnson successfully brought his Great Society into being.

Johnson motivated a federal assumption of several new obligations to the disenfranchised. Newly established Medicare and Medicaid programs paired with substantial enhancements to social security established a new standard for the welfare state. The tax burden and the bureaucratic paperwork established to support this Great Society legislation imposed substantial constraints on all entrepreneurial enterprises. Small businesses that had been the main engine fueling the economic growth of America began to buckle under the weight of the paperwork of federal mandates and the related tax obligations. By the end of the 1960s, it is very evident that concept of personal freedoms within a free-enterprise economy was beginning to fade.

The next event worthy of note is the presidency of Jimmy Carter. President Carter did not establish any significant new social welfare programs of note. He did, however, establish a means of reducing the heavy national debt stemming from the funding of Medicare and Medicaid— double digit inflation. Inflation became the tool Carter, his administration, and Congress used to kick the (social security and Medicare financing) can down the road.

The final death knell for free enterprise rang in 2008. Obama won the presidential election, inheriting an economic meltdown stemming from a worldwide failure in the financial services industry. Potential bank failures created a situation strangely similar to FDR's first days in office (soon after being sworn in, FDR was forced to declare a bank holiday to save the banks). Leveraging the fear and uncertainty stemming from the worst economic downturn since the Great Depression, Obama and the Democrat-controlled Congress led by Nancy Pelosi pounced on the opportunity to eliminate most of the remaining elements of the free-enterprise system. Using bailout funds provided by a Democrat-controlled Congress, Obama established substantial federal control over segments of the economy that had stubbornly clung to their independence. New legislation provided substantial federal control over economic segments that had somehow escaped substantial oversight throughout the progressive revolution. Banking, Wall Street, insurance, health care, and auto manufacturing had successfully remained private-sector businesses. All immediately faced substantial federal regulatory restrictions and control following the Obama election.

With Obama's election and the coattail electoral victories by the Democrats (allowing them full control of Congress), big government finally gained the political capital to step in and take control of the health care delivery system, Wall Street, the auto industry, and investment banking. More bureaucracy, more control, and more taxes. Years of selling progressive ideology to the middle class finally convinced the majority of Americans that federal bureaucrats are more capable of fairly managing the business of America than the private-sector business owner. Leveraging the panic arising out of the economic collapse, Obama sized the opportunity, much like FDR did.

Fear and panic allowed him to successfully push through legislation that established federal control of the health care industry. What is now referred to as Obamacare has set the groundwork for nationalizing the industry. National health care is sure to follow. In the span of a few short months, Obama and his congressional Democrats seized control of the remaining aspects of American life that had been overlooked by the New Deal and Great Society.

Today, the massive federal bureaucracy is strangling the life out of the American main-street businessman. Economic opportunity, originally available to all, is now limited to only those massive companies that are capable of employing an army of professionals who are capable of understanding and complying with the extensive volume of laws and regulations relating to their chosen endeavor.

Socially responsible big government, launched with a vengeance during the Franklin Roosevelt administration, is now permanently embedded. The overwhelming financial burden created by big-government entitlements combined with all the related social controls and business regulations is crushing the free-enterprise system. The massive bureaucracy formed to administer the New Deal has never diminished. Federal entitlement programs like social security and Medicare have proven to be dependent upon an ever-increasing level of taxation to survive. Escalating taxes are removing more and more funds from the free-flow economy. Significant amounts of revenue that could have been reinvested and recirculated are now being usurped by America's big-government entitlements. The typical business owner pays multiple layers of state and federal taxation to finance the core elements of our socially responsible "nanny state." These taxes are gobbling up free cash flow like Pac-Man.

The founding fathers' version of a free-enterprise economy is gone. It has passed into history just like the free-range environment of the American Indians. Statutory requirements to provide health insurance, workers' compensation coverage, unemployment insurance, FICA and Medicare contributions, licensing fees and license requirements, business permits, OSHA requirements, along with myriads of other business taxes and surcharges (buried in items like their health insurance premiums) drain most of the time, energy, and free cash flow available to the small businessman. The entrepreneurs' time spent complying with regulations, completing forms, and keeping up with regulations replaces much of the time that could have been spent growing their businesses. Money formerly used to grow and expand the business enterprise is now spent on employee-benefit mandates and taxes. Main-street businessmen are closing their doors, lamenting that it is no longer worth the effort.

Let's share a story that illustrates the changes that have occurred over the past century—a story about an Irish immigrant, Tommy Dowdall, who left his ancestral home to immigrate to America in 1908.

Tommy was only nineteen when he boarded the ship to America, carrying only a small suitcase that held in its contents all that he owned. He took his life savings, fifteen dollars converted from English pounds, and another five dollars given to him by his mother, along with two pairs of haircutting shears that composed his tools of the trade.

Tommy's mother was a well-respected small-town hairdresser who had taught Tommy all she knew when he showed interest and ability when we was only fourteen. By the time he turned sixteen, Tommy had established his own group of regular customers. He set appointments with his clients and traveled to the customer's home to cut hair. His clients were poor and inclined to cut their own hair, using Tommy infrequently, mostly for special events. He had no opportunity in Ireland to fully support himself in the hair trade. He jumped at the chance to immigrate to New York once a former client wrote him a letter and invited him to stay with his family in their New York apartment. A few weeks after receiving the letter, Tommy was boarding the ship and on his way.

He arrived in New York seasick, homesick, and dumfounded by the enormity of New York City. He successfully located his former client and moved into a small, three-room second-floor apartment that was home to his friend, his friend's wife, her mother, and his client's four children. Tommy was given a small corner of the kitchen to sleep in and a small cupboard that he shared with one of the children to store his personal belongings. Tommy's share of the rent was two dollars a week, so he wasn't going to last long in New York unless he found work. Fortunately, his former client had issued the invitation knowing that Tommy had a trade that could sustain him in New York. Word was out that Tommy had exceptional skill at hairdressing, and his first clients were in his chair in the kitchen of the apartment within the first week.

Soon Tommy had a regular flow of clients coming to the house for their hair appointments. Word was out; Tommy was exceptional and affordable. His big break came when we was summoned to the home of a wealthy New York socialite whose daughter was about to be married. He was offered twenty dollars to do the hair for the wedding party on the morning of the wedding. Big money, big opportunity. The results were fantastic, and once everyone found out who did their hair, Tommy was the toast of the town.

Attracting and retaining wealthy clients depended upon the existence of a well-furnished beauty shop easily accessible to the potential clientele. Tommy risked all he had to rent a small shop near Park Avenue. Clients flocked in, and soon Tommy's appointment book was full. He was turning people away, as he had no time for new clients!

At this point, Tommy took another big risk. He chose an apprentice—a young, attractive Italian immigrant who displayed extraordinary skill. He brought her in as an assistant to help book appointments and help with the simple cuts. Soon she mastered the trade and was attracting clients at a pace equal to Tommy. Within a few months, she was handling as many clients as Tommy.

Tommy's salon was now the highest-profile shop in New York. He had no difficulty attracting the best hairdressers in the city. Keeping true to his roots, Tommy began hiring and training a number of recently arrived immigrants. Business was booming, and Tommy was becoming a wealthy man. He soon had salons in several prime New York locations. Managing the operations combined with the time requirements needed for recruiting and training new hairdressers was taking all of his available time, taking him away from his true passion, hairstyling.

Tommy, a country boy at heart, always felt uncomfortable in New York City—too many people, too little fresh air. He wanted land and wanted to get back to hairstyling. He decided to sell the business and move to the country. Taking the enormous profits from selling all the salons, Tommy purchased a large farm in Western Pennsylvania and then opened a small salon in town where he worked three days a week. Only twenty-eight and wealthy beyond his wildest dreams, he was set for life.

What would have happened to Tommy had our current environment existed back in 1908?

First of all, Tommy would need to complete paperwork to obtain a visa required if he intended to move to America. He would then have to wait for that process to be approved. The visa he would receive would be deemed temporary. He could come to America on a temporary basis and would then have to apply for citizenship to stay permanently.

Fire codes and housing requirements would have prevented Tommy from moving in with his former client.

Tommy could not pursue his hairdressing career until he was fully licensed. Licensing would require a specific number of hours of education, passing the requisite exams, and applying and paying for his license. All of which would have taken time and money.

Zoning requirements would probably restrict Tommy from conducting his business from his apartment (assuming he rented one). He likely would need to apply for a chair in an existing salon to start his business. He would likely need the services of an attorney to assist in forming his business entity, acquire a tax identification number, and obtain a business certificate from New York State. More time, more money.

His agreement to rent a chair in an existing salon would likely restrict him from hiring any additional hairstylists. Should he wish to expand and hire additional stylists, he would likely be required to terminate his existing agreement (hopefully the existing salon did not make him sign a noncompete agreement).

Once he decided to open his own salon, he would likely be required to obtain a lease that required at least a one-month deposit and a lease duration of at least a year. He would then be required to provide proof of insurance coverage and would have to purchase and finance all of his own furnishings and equipment. His lack of capital would require him to acquire some type of financing (if he managed to qualify). Good luck in today's environment finding a bank willing to make a loan to an energetic entrepreneur with no capital and no track record.

To hire his first employee, he would likely need a to hire a payroll-processing company to perform all the payroll deductions and employer reporting requirements in place to account for required FICA, Medicare, unemployment, and federal and state withholding. He would also be required to purchase workers' compensation insurance, New York disability insurance, and soon Obamacare, health insurance.

As the business expanded, Tommy would be required to comply with a myriad of regulations: workers' compensation laws, OSHA, ERISA, Americans with Disabilities Act, HIPPA, and many, many others. His business would face so many potential liabilities that Tommy would often feel he was under assault from the legal profession, hordes of attorneys seeking an opportunity to attach punitive penalties for every misstep the business may take. Potential liabilities could come from every aspect of his business: professional liability (from clients unhappy with outcomes), employment practices liability (discrimination, failure to promote, improper dismissal, etc.), premises slips and falls, products liability, employee benefits liability, fiduciary liability for the company's employee retirement plan, pollution liability, advertising liability, liable, slander, defamation of character, cyber liability (from his online client information), and many other undefined exposures.

Laws have been passed that also would require Tommy to verify citizenship of each new employee, verify proper tax reporting for his subcontracted hairstylists, and make quarterly deposits of his own income taxes sufficient to cover his potential tax liabilities. He would also have to deal with sales tax collection and reporting, employee wage garnishments, discriminatory practices in employee benefit plans, licensing requirements, including continuing education, handicap access to his premises, product disposal/pollution exposures, credit card processing, banking relationships, mortgage regulations, and thousands of other responsibilities that may (or may not) have an impact on his business. Tommy would face an unending volume of business regulations that an untrained immigrant from Ireland would never have the education or experience to comprehend.

Assume Tommy found his way through the matrix of laws and regulations and still managed to build a successful business. At age twenty-eight, he accepted an offer to sell his business, hoping to take the proceeds and buy a farm in Western Pennsylvania. Unfortunately, he first had to pay his attorney and accountant for closing the deal and final reporting of Tommy's total capital gain on the business sale. Then he had to pay his state and federal capital gains tax. His advisors also encouraged him to deposit some of the proceeds into a tax-advantaged retirement plan. They also encouraged him to engage another professional to assist in developing an estate plan to help his potential heirs avoid paying some of the potential state and federal estate taxes (as much as 50 percent of the estate value) that would be due within a year should anything happen to cause Tommy's death. By the time he was done with the taxes, fees, deferrals, and estate plans, Tommy had insufficient cash available to purchase his farm. He needed a thirty-year mortgage to purchase the farm of his dreams and had to take a full-time position in town as a much sought-out hairstylist to pay the mortgage.

Many Americans are asking, how did this happen? Why did it happen? Should it have happened? What was the tipping point that changed America? Who was responsible and why did we let it happen? Those who understand the extent of the changes will ask the biggest question of all: where do we go from here?

Creation of Freefare is the logical next step! Freefare is the future, the *ultimate level* of socially responsible federal entitlement programs: the fully mature form of government assistance in the age of entitlement. Freefare is exactly where our big-government, bleeding-heart politicians are leading us. Not to be confused with welfare (governmental support for those who *cannot work*), Freefare is governmental support for not only those citizens who cannot find work but also those who *do not want to work*. Finally the politicians can dispose of the burden to prove a disability or the unavailability of work as a basis of enrollment.

In the Freefare future, anyone can declare a need, and the government will take care of him or her. Political leaders will embrace Freefare as a system in which federal bureaucrats can control every aspect of the lives of all who are enrolled. Freefare will be very appealing to our political leaders as it will become the ultimate means to control the have-not social segment, completely removing them as a potential threat to society. Government will be able to monitor and manage every aspect of Freefare existence: nutrition, clothing, location, alcohol and drug consumption, medical care, education, and entertainment—the full realization of the nanny state. It will be sold to the working man/woman (in exchange for their vote) under the guise of safety and security.

Over the past several decades, the politicians from both parties have been elevating the expectations of the bottom tier of society. There is no turning back. We can reminisce about the free-enterprise world created by the founding fathers, but that world is gone. The only way to revert back to free enterprise is to stage another revolution, and that is never going to happen. The only affordable path forward is Freefare. Let's put the cards on the table and call it what it is—full support for those who will not or cannot provide for themselves, efficient redistribution of wealth to bridge the gap between the wealthy and the poor. The federal government can create an affordable means to take care of the needy by consolidating all programs, eliminating the bureaucracy, and just giving them what they need. Once instituted, Freefare will lead us to a truly classless society. Socially, very little will exist that differentiates those that work and achieve from those that do not labor to sustain a quality lifestyle. Read on! See the future!

CHAPTER 4

The American Progressive Movement

Let's start with a detailed review of the historical sequence of events that transformed America from a free-enterprise democracy into a socially responsible welfare state.

If one were to study the free-enterprise American experiment, they would commence their studies by examining the philosophical debates between Alexander Hamilton (favoring federal social responsibility, manufacturing, and a strong national system of banking and government) and Thomas Jefferson (favoring local social responsibility, agriculture, and state's rights). Strong federal oversight, Hamilton argued, would create an economy unencumbered by a myriad of state tariffs and trade restrictions. Jefferson favored local oversight in what was primarily an agrarian society. Their debates set the stage for the American two-party system. The Hamilton Federalists, promoting federal oversight, challenged Jefferson's Republicans, who favored limited local control. Republicans feared the Federalists would soon destroy the democracy, causing America to revert to a monocracy. Would the American experiment survive? Responding to the leadership of the founding fathers (and in particular George Washington), compromise was reached. Balance between states' rights and federal oversight was achieved, and the free-enterprise economy began to flourish.

The French Revolution had introduced the guillotine as a tool to enforce the will of the masses. Prior to their revolution, the majority of the French wealth was in the hands of the titled nobility. The vast majority of the French population was impoverished and suffering. The titled nobility, protecting their superior economic status, effectively ignored the demands being made by the masses to grant the common man a voice in the government. The starving French commoners, realizing they had nothing to lose, massed in force to *withdraw their consent.* They efficiently used the guillotine to impose their will. The American Revolution had sparked a flame in the hearts and minds of the lower class that ignited a full-fledged conflagration in Paris. The common Frenchman fully embraced the concept of consent of the governed articulated in the American Declaration of Independence. Once their passions were ignited, there was no stopping the French inferno.

By the early 1820s, it became clear that the initial experiment in democracy had succeeded even though France continued to struggle with the concept. The American democracy remained open to all who could reach its shores. The economy was exploding, buoyed by the positive effects of unrestrained immigration. Millions of new Americans, energized by the high hope generated from the opportunity to directly benefit from the fruits of their labor, were flooding our shores. They were coming to a new world that offered everyone the opportunity to lift themselves from extreme poverty. Most came to America with little more than the coins in their pockets and the clothes on their backs. They left home and took a giant risk, without the benefit of a safety net and without any guarantees. They came for the opportunity. Every citizen was given the chance to build wealth and establish financial security. Most immigrants landing at Ellis Island mortgaged their future to get to America. Their reward was the opportunity to gain financial security equal to the established aristocracy back in the Old World. The promise of America was enormous economic opportunity within a framework of a tolerant, nonintrusive government. Existing federal taxes in the early 1800s were extremely limited, applying primarily to imports. Government intrusion into the business world was intentionally restricted to a handful of state and local regulations. American business was free to grow uninhibited from restrictive regulation, and the economy flourished.

The next chapter in American economic history advances past the Civil War to the later 1800s. This period was filled with explosive growth, inventive ingenuity with unlimited opportunity, and the arrival of the American industrialist. An ambitious man could go from the farm fields of America's undeveloped frontier and become one of the world's greatest leaders (Abraham Lincoln). Students would read about the fantastic wealth that came to those who were willing to pioneer new industries (Rockefeller in oil and railroads, Carnegie in steel, Ford in automobiles), the rise of the American industrialist. America became an economic giant, dominating all other world economies. In a mere 120 years, America went from a cluster of small Atlantic coast settlements to the greatest nation on earth, fueled by the unfettered opportunities and personal freedoms offered in the new nation.

Shortly after the start of the twentieth century, world attitudes began to transform. The working class had commenced a long, hard struggle to establish their fair share of economic opportunity. Civilization began to abandon the concept of rugged individualism in favor of a softer, gentler, liberal approach to social responsibility. In Russia and Europe, socialism was on the rise.

Progressivism began to take root in America. The election of Woodrow Wilson, who campaigned as a progressive Democrat, confirmed the extent of the change. Wilson, the affable college professor, promised social reform. Once inaugurated, he immediately initiated substantial progressive reforms. The advent of World War I and the resulting destruction of the Austrian empire accelerated the global progressive transition. Wilson's initiatives (especially the income tax) were the initial indication that the grand American free-enterprise experiment had reached maturity and was following a new path.

Globally, this time frame spanning from 1915 to 1930 was a revolutionary period marked by global political upheaval. The longstanding well-established monarchies began to feel insecure about the future. The ruling class accustomed to asserting authority without resistance sought the means to reconfirm their power and authority. Ultimately, the monarchal fear and political insecurity led to onset of World War I. The mess that ensued reinforced within the general populace the need for change.

The post–World War I economic collapse in Germany and Russia set the stage for a meaningful turn in each country's political philosophy. Each movement faced the same challenge—how best to recover funds from the wealthy and use those funds to finance support of the underprivileged. The process of redistributing wealth within each country was approached differently. However, the goal was the same: find a way to force the wealthy to subsidize the welfare of the poor.

The Russian czar's willingness to callously sacrifice thousands of peasants in the World War I battlefields provided the catalyst for the Russian revolution. Poverty in Russia had been accepted as a way of life. Isolated and unaware of the conditions that existed in Europe and America, the Russian peasant tended to accept his or her lot in life. Living conditions in the major cities were atrocious. Factory workers resided in city slums in dilapidated tenement buildings, often having several families sharing small apartments. Men and women trudged to the factories and were forced to work in hostile environments at a wage that barley allowed survival. Country peasants were uneducated and ill-treated. Most could not read or write and were so totally isolated they may as well have been residing on another planet. Slowly, starting in major cities like Moscow and St. Petersburg, the concepts of collective bargaining and unionization were beginning to seep in. Small victories gave rise to hope. Hope gave rise to confidence. Then Karl Marx issued his *Communist Manifesto*. Concepts expressed in the manifesto were fully embraced by the suppressed working class, and soon the Russian proletariat began to organize. Bolshevism was on the rise. All the movement needed was a catalyst to crystallize the brotherhood. The decision by the czar to enter WWI acted as that catalyst. His callous willingness to send his peasants to slaughter was the final act. Czar Nicholas lost the hearts and minds of the proletariat, and the consent of the governed began to collapse. The advent of World War I and the writings of Karl Marx soon gave birth to the Russian revolution.

The Russian revolution set the wheels in motion. The Bolsheviks rose to power, advocating the concept of worker equality. Promising governance based upon political consent of the masses (as was being done in America), the Bolsheviks were successful in overthrowing centuries of oppression imposed by the Russian monarchy. The rise of the proletariat and the fall of the czar sent a shudder through the European aristocracy. Russia's regal form of government that had existed for centuries was forcibly overthrown, and the starving masses murdered the czar and his entire family to assure that none were left to restore power. Most of the remaining Russian aristocracy either fled the country or were sent to Siberia. Once the deed was done, the riotous proletariat collectivized as Bolsheviks. Their leaders secured power by promising relief from economic suffering to be achieved by sharing the massive land holding formerly held by the ruling class. Everything was to be community owned (commune style) and equally shared, thus the term *communist*. Unschooled in the intricacies of community sharing (democracy), the proletariat had no clue how to proceed with the process of establishing a government capable of maintaining the consent of the governed. Lenin rose to power as a totalitarian dictator, and unlike America's first president, George Washington, he intended to remain in power for the balance of his life.

Upon Lenin's death, Joseph Stalin grabbed the reins of power. He too had no intention of ever relinquishing his position. To secure his authority, he set about exterminating all who opposed Communism (him), and hundreds of thousands died. In concept, the Russian Communist Party was intended to be a policing force whose mission was to equalize society through forcible redistribution of wealth and economic recourses. In reality, the USSR, especially under Stalin, was a harsh dictatorship secured by the secret police. Political consent of the masses was implied, and those who objected were either exterminated or sent to Siberia.

In Germany, the Fascist Party gained control, offering an alternate approach to the regal form of government. The economically challenged Germans embraced the hope for a fairer means of wealth redistribution the Fascist Party offered.

In America, the process evolved in a more civilized manner. The populist revolution started with the acceptance of the income tax as the primary source of federal revenue. Imposing significant taxes upon those earning high incomes to finance reform appeared to be a far more acceptable alternative to wealth redistribution when compared to what had occurred in Russia or Germany. Wilson had sold it to Congress as a temporary measure to finance World War I. Congressional approval faced little opposition. A progressive majority in Congress embraced the patriotic approach of taxing the wealthy, generating a significant increase in federal revenue. Few opposed the tax, as it applied only to the wealthy and was instituted only to finance the war. Economic times were good, and many businessmen were benefiting from the surge in manufacturing arising from the demand to generate war material. Why not require those with significant incomes, benefiting from the American war effort, to give back to the government? This change to a federal income tax exclusively levied on the wealthy class, expressly imposed to generate increased federal revenue, was a significant change of direction for the American free-enterprise democracy.

Once the Wilson-era legislators implemented the tax and spend process to finance their war efforts, they inadvertently uncovered the road to future societal control. As soon as Congress recognized the vast social engineering opportunities the income tax represented, they were not about to repeal it. The amazing flow of tax revenue appealed to every member of Congress. They were salivating over the opportunities the flow of tax revenue represented. All that remained was to determine how far the tax rate could be pushed.

The new Wilson income tax applied to only high-wage earners and left a vast majority of lower-income eligible voters exempt; therefore, the newly imposed income tax was viewed by most working Americans as a fair and equitable method of financing government programs. In reality, it was America's first experiment with devising a peaceful means of redistributing wealth. It met with little or no opposition. From this point on, creating and collecting income taxes evolved into the universally accepted means of redistributing American wealth.

The shift toward social reform and the age of entitlement began only months after America had reached its 150th birthday. The innovative concepts used to establish America's free-market democratic society were gradually compromised through congressional legislation never contemplated in the Constitution. America embarked on a path that would abandon the free-enterprise experiment as the federal government succumbed to the rise of the proletariat. Our founding fathers are all weeping in their graves. Lenin, Trotsky, and Marx, the founders of Russian Communism, are exalting in their tombs, comforted in the victory of their beloved proletariat over the hated capitalists (all three wondering why *they* didn't promote the peaceful, prolonged evolutionary approach to establish "economic equality for all" rather than creating a system that endorsed the violent repression of their constituents). Karl Marx would tell you the progressive evolution of America was an inevitable consequence of the conflict between free enterprise and Communism. His theory of dialectic materialism worked to perfection. The enduring battles waged between free enterprise and Communism altered both, giving rise to a new theory of government, *enlightened socialism.*

Jay Winik's novel *The Great Upheaval* clearly documents worldwide events occurring during the period of 1788 to 1800. Winik outlines concurrent global events that gave rise to the modern world. In the book, Winik ties what seem to be unrelated events together and graphically demonstrates that they were not isolated, unrelated occurrences. The events—the American Revolution, the French Revolution, and the reign of Catherine the Great in Russia—were all related to a global change in political philosophy. They all resulted from the evolution of philosophical change in the theory of government, the theory that governments exist at the consent of the governed.

I suggest the second great upheaval occurred during the period 1917–32. The Russian revolution, the rise of Fascism, and the progressive movement in America all resulted from another philosophical change—the belief that all governments existing at the consent of the governed must also guarantee a minimum quality of life for everyone under their jurisdiction.

How did the suffering masses successfully alter the primary premise of government and eliminate monarchal control? World War I was the catalyst. The commencement of World War I marked the end of the power held by the Old World ruling class. The enormity of the conflict had a significant economic impact on all who participated. The European continent became an entrenched battlefield few could escape. Monarchal control of central Europe began to dissolve shortly after the Austrian empire collapsed. The fighting was brutal, and the loss of life was staggering. The length and breadth of the conflict caused the general populace to reconsider how they were governed and why they were killing each other.

American participation in World War I marked the end of American adolescence. Prior decades had focused on America's manifest destiny, America's youthful exuberance to occupy the continent from sea to shining sea. The establishment of new continental territories and transitioning those territories into states quickly admitted to the union consumed every ounce of our youthful energy. All focus was inward. From the time Daniel Boone crossed over the Allegany Mountains through the Cumberland Gap, revealing the riches held in the vast wilderness, Americans became obsessed with westward migration. New opportunity lay just across the next river or just beyond the next mountain ridge. Those who felt disenfranchised in the original thirteen states poured through the Cumberland Gap, or down the Ohio River, or over the Great Lakes, to stake their claim on the future. The human flood consumed everything in its path. Native Americans were pushed aside, their way of life lost in the human tsunami. Even the daunting Rocky Mountains failed to stem the tide. President James K. Polk sealed the deal with the American acquisition of Texas and California as a reward for engaging in a conflict with Mexico. By the time of the California gold rush in 1849, it was clear that the continent from the Canadian border to the newly redesigned Mexican border now belonged to America. All who participated in the westward migration could have cared less about the political upheaval on the other side of the Atlantic. Europe was an ocean and a generation away.

All this youthful innocence ended with the election of Woodrow Wilson and his decision to enter the European conflict, World War I.

PART 2

The Path to Freefare

America begins the evolution from free enterprise to socialism as the capitalists' greed leads them to consolidate business ventures into multistate trusts formed to eliminate competition and control prices and wages. The American working man embraces the emerging progressive political movement to combat the influence of the massive business trusts.

CHAPTER 5

Woodrow Wilson

Early in the second decade of the twentieth century, America elected as its president Woodrow Wilson, former president of Princeton University. Wilson campaigned for the presidency as a progressive Democrat promising a federal government committed to taking care of Americans. He was the first presidential candidate to use a campaign slogan indicating that Americans needed to be cared for! American progressivism was on the rise, gaining strength from the flood of European and Russian immigrants arriving from venues that would soon give support to Fascists and Communists. His campaign against the Republican incumbent, William Taft, and former president, Teddy Roosevelt, running on the third party Bull Moose ticket, became one of the great contests in American history.

Wilson first gained national attention with his book *History of American People.* His lecture tour in support of the book appealed to many Americans. Democrats long seeking a viable national candidate took note. Since the Civil War, the Democrats had been wandering in the wilderness regarding the presidency. The party had become a party of the South. Tainted by secession and rebellion, they had a very difficult time fielding credible national candidates, Grover Cleveland being the only exception. Wilson's professorial manner and talent for public speaking drew a considerable amount of national attention. The national Democrats took note and chose to test his electability by convincing him to run for governor of New Jersey in 1910. He won in a landslide, besting his Republican opponent by a two to one margin. This set the stage to represent the party in the presidential campaign in 1912, which he won once he gained the support of William Jennings Bryant.

Wilson couldn't compete with Teddy Roosevelt on the Rough Rider's terms and knew not to try. Wilson's approach was cooler and more cerebral yet inspired by a passion of his own. The compelling question of the day, he said, was what to do about the trusts, the corporate combines that appeared to be squeezing the life out of business competition all while exhorting excessive profits from the American people. Standard Oil's solicitor general, Samuel C.T. Dodd, devised the corporate trust in 1881 to help John D. Rockefeller improve control over Standard Oil. The corporate trust then quickly evolved to become the standard format for most large businesses. The early history of these trusts became associated with abusive practices as the large entities held by the trust frequently used their size to exclude competition. Teddy Roosevelt also assailed the trusts, but where Roosevelt wanted to rein in the trusts by regulating them, Wilson demanded their destruction, their breakup into small entities that would have to compete for the customer's favor rather than dictate the terms on which they would deal with the customers. He waged an all-out assault. Wilson told a Detroit audience, "What I am interested in is laws that will give the little man a start, that will give him a chance to show these fellows that he has brains enough to compete with them and can presently make his local market a national market, a world market and put them to their mettle to do the business more intelligently and economically and systematically than he can."[7] Once the dust settled, Wilson's New Freedom campaign won by a sizable margin. He won in the electoral college with 435 votes compared to Roosevelt's eighty-eight and Taft's eight, a clear voter mandate to proceed with his progressive initiatives.

True to his word, using his electoral mandate, Wilson opened his presidential term with an aggressive antitrust effort promising to break up business monopolies. His first primary target for reform was the banking industry. He firmly believed the industry was the root cause of most national economic and social problems, believing most bankers were controlled by the wealthy industrialists who were suppressing competition and creating monopolies. Wilson stated during the summer of 1913, "The control of the system of banking … must be public not private, must be vested in the government itself, so that banks may be the instruments, not the masters, of business and of individual enterprise and initiative."[8]

He pressed hard to achieve this vital plank in his progressive platform. However, the bankers, wealthy industrialists, and their political allies threw up hurdle after hurdle to defeat the president's plan. Many of the plan's opponents felt Wilson's approach was a move toward socialism. In the end, the essence of Wilson's reform initiative prevailed though a series of compromises that caused it to

---

[7] *Woodrow Wilson*, The American Presidents Series, Times Books, page 21.

[8] Address to Joint Session June 23, 1913.

fall short of his goal to nationalize the banks. Two days before Christmas 1913, a political compromise presented President Wilson with the Federal Reserve Act, proposed legislation that essentially achieved his goal of controlling the power of the banks. He immediately signed the act. The new act left ownership of the banks in private hands but vested oversight in a board appointed by the president, the Federal Reserve Board.

The Federal Reserve Board struggled at first but has since evolved into a key component of the American economic system. It is important to understand that the Federal Reserve is not a federal agency; it is a privately owned entity governed by a federally appointed board of directors. It would be a worthwhile effort for all readers to research the actual inner workings of the Federal Reserve, an institution that has established itself as America's primary overseer of financial activity.

Wilson's progressive momentum was soon halted as America was drawn into World War I. German attacks on oceangoing shipping became the issue that turned the tide. Wilson issued stern warnings that any future attacks on ships carrying American passengers would bring retaliation. The Germans initially agreed to cease the attacks, but once they restarted, Wilson had no choice but to enter the war.

Shortly after America entered the conflict, a significant event occurred that signaled the beginning of the end of free enterprise—a congressional act that would have significant impact on all future generations. Hoping to pay for as much of the war as possible without borrowing, Wilson persuaded Congress to temporarily establish an individual income tax and supplement those income taxes with an excess profits tax and other levies. The results were remarkable. Prior to the war, three-quarters of federal revenues were derived from the tariff and excise taxes on vices such as alcohol and tobacco. After the war, three-quarters came from income and estate taxes.

"Whatever else they thought of the war, progressives had to concede that the conflict was a powerful engine for tax reform, putting into practice the progressive idea that those most able to pay should in fact pay the most."[9]

Future politicians would discover that it could be used as a tool to equalize the social environment and limit the accumulation of wealth simply by determining *how much was enough* and *who was wealthy*. Emerging progressives armed with this effective tool to cap the earnings of successful businessmen immediately began to erode the foundation of the free enterprise economy.

Labeling the income tax a temporary step was a stroke of genius. It was easy to pass and appealed to the majority of patriotic Americans.

Liberal politicians found it easy to increase the tax base simply by expanding the definition of wealth. Empowered to impose taxes on individual earnings (and later to also grant deductions to reduce taxable income). motivated politicians soon discovered the income tax could be used to establish a form of control over most individual economic activities. The design and implementation of tax deductions (such as interest on mortgages) provides the means to encourage certain activities (such as home buying) deemed worthwhile to society as a whole.

The physiological impact the income tax had on wealthy Americans is rarely discussed. Prior to the Wilson income tax, America's phenomenal economic growth was fueled by

---

[9] *Woodrow Wilson*, The American Presidents Series, Times Books, page 83.

entrepreneurial industrialists like Carnegie, Rockefeller, and Ford, who flourished in an economic environment that was essentially unregulated and untaxed. Personal and corporate income taxes did not exist. What would have happened to Ford Motor Company or Standard Oil had the government been able to erode their capital with income tax? Would Carnegie, Rockefeller, and Henry Ford have found offshore vehicles to direct their corporate profits to? Instead of reinvesting a substantial portion of their untaxed personal earnings, these entrepreneurs would have probably found it more efficient to move their wealth to safer tax-preferred investments, limiting the stream of income that went back into their business ventures. The lost income likely would have deprived the free-enterprise economic engine of much of its needed fuel. Millions of dollars that was used to expand the American industrialists' business ventures would have been siphoned off to fund tax obligations and tax-avoidance vehicles, resulting in slower expansion and slower job growth. By the end of the Roaring Twenties, escalating personal and business taxes would indeed become one of the contributing causes of the economic slowdown that led to the Great Depression.

The implementation of substantial income taxes marks the first step toward a totally new concept of government: the concept that a key function of all governments is to oversee a fair and equitable distribution of wealth.

After the war, President Woodrow Wilson's wholehearted support of the League of Nations (the predecessor of the United Nations) confirmed a new commitment to the global community. He wanted to export American ideals, thus making the world a safer place. During this period, America began turning its focus from an inward bias (manifest destiny) to a global focus. In a speech on September 19, 1918,

Wilson framed the core issue that would draw America into the global community:

> Shall the military power of any nation or group of nations be suffered to determine the fortunes of peoples over whom they have no right to rule except the right of force? Shall strong nations be free to wrong weak nations and make them subject to their purpose and interest? Shall peoples be ruled and dominated, even in their own internal affairs, by arbitrary and responsible force or their own will and choice? Shall there be a common standard of right and privilege for all peoples and nations, or shall the strong do as they will and weak suffer without redress.[10]

Wilson was determined to form a global police force intended to prevent strong nations from imposing their wills on weaker nations. The European community had embraced America's participation in the war and greatly appreciated Wilson's leadership in the post war negotiations. The European leaders, initially skeptical of the effort to form a global policing mechanism, relented in the wake of Wilson's immense popularity with their constituents. Though his dream of a global acceptance of the League of Nations failed to take hold in America, the expectation of American protection was firmly in place. America could no longer hide within its own borders even though the majority of Americans wished to remain isolated. The world was now

---

[10] Address, September 27, 1918.

expecting America to step in and protect the sovereignty of all nations no matter how weak or small. The financial obligations tied to global crisis management intended to avoid any major international conflicts would soon become a major drain on the federal budget.

By the time Wilson left office, he had inspired dramatic change in the American political landscape. America emerged from the war not only as a world-class military power but also as the primary participant in a global police force. Europe embraced American authority and Wilson's concept of protectionism. America was now the primary player on the worldwide political stage. The emerging bureaucracy, growing military, and international financial obligations were financed through a national income tax while the economy was supported by a managed monetary system controlled by the newly established Federal Reserve.

Wilson's term as president was the most impactful term since Abraham Lincoln's. He dramatically changed the country in the eight-year span of his presidency. During his two terms, he did the following:

1) He institutionalized the first elements of federal control over the national economy with the creation of the Federal Reserve.
2) He initiated the first steps toward meaningful wealth distribution, initiating the federal income tax as America's civilized method of wealth redistribution.
3) Finally, he successfully positioned America as the primary global enforcer of national protectionism.

The stage was set for more taxation, greater regulation, and the commencement of America's substantial financial commitment to international peace management.

CHAPTER 6

Roosevelt's New Deal

The decade following World War I, the decade spanning 1920–30, was a Republican-dominated American transition period, falling between Democrats Woodrow Wilson and FDR. Republicans were in charge throughout the decade, and they were determined to keep the size and scope of the federal government under control. Under conservative Republican leadership, America withdrew from the European mess, and most Americans were relishing isolation. The economy was booming. Free enterprise was functioning at its best. Jobs were plentiful, money was flowing, everybody was prospering, and there was no need for more progressive reform.

Over 150 years of laissez-faire economics brought us to the 1920s, the Roaring Twenties. The economy was booming. America's entry into World War I had given American farmers and manufacturers a worldwide market for their products. Business owners and farmers were completely unrestrained by federal regulation or excessive taxes. Everyone was prospering. Every individual who wanted work could find a job. New businesses were popping up everywhere. The automobile industry was exploding, creating factory jobs at a pace never seen before. Farmers were prosperous, benefiting from the substitution of American farm produce for European produce devastated by the war.

As the Roaring Twenties drew to a close, the opportunity for the American progressive/socialist movement to take over came with the advent of the Great Depression. Most historians want to blame America's Great Depression on President Herbert Hoover and his conservative hands-off view of the economy. While it is true that Hoover did little to stop the American economic slide, historically there was no established precedence in the free-enterprise world to indicate the federal government could or should step in and supplement the flow of the economy whenever the normal business cycle turned negative. In fairness to Hoover, he also had very few resources at his disposal to turn the economic tide. The federal government Hoover presided over was amazingly limited in scope. The entire federal budget in 1929 was under $4 billion of which over $1 billion (over 25 percent) was being paid out as veterans' benefits to World War I veterans. Hoover had limited resources to battle the recession, and he was philosophically opposed to altering the role of the federal bureaucracy. Historically welfare was the responsibility of the states not the federal government.

Severe recessions had occurred before. Despite the success of the free-enterprise system, the American economy had suffered several in the 1800s. Presidential leadership throughout that period resisted the temptation to step in and take control of the economy. In fact presidents like Andrew Jackson refused to take economic control even in the face of severe economic downturns, such as the one created when the National Bank cut off lending in response to President Jackson's threats to veto the renewal of the bank's charter.

Jackson feared federal consolidation of power and control of the economy. His biggest issue was the economic power of a National Bank. He spent most of his political capital fighting the central bank's power over the economy.

A number of other presidents were also forced to deal with recessions. Most recognized that economic downturns are a fundamental element of a free-enterprise economy. Corrections are a necessity to assure the proper evolution of the system. Survival of the fittest leads to the elimination of older, useless enterprises in favor of new establishments embracing new products and services. Often the retooling of the economy causes economic hardships. The transition cannot be successful if the weak are subsidized and allowed to survive merely to sustain an outdated failing enterprise. Prior to the Great Depression, all presidents allowed the economy to run its course. Federal economic stimulus was avoided. All believed the economy would recover on its own.

At the end of the 1920s, the abundance of greed, ignorance, and apathy combined to turn the lights off on the boom times. Four events occurred over a very short period of time and combined to start the downhill slide that signaled the onset of American economic collapse:

1) England abandoned the gold standard, causing worldwide economic uncertainty. England's decision to abandon the gold standard opened the door to substantially inflating the English pound. Staggering under the debt incurred in fighting the war, the English had to find a way out. The gold standard had tied the pound to the worldwide value of gold, stabilizing it against other monetary currencies (like the American dollar). It served as a base monetary value that prevented any

substantial inflation. Removing the gold standard would allow the pound to inflate in proportion to the government's willingness to print currency. Inflating the pound would provide an easy means to reduce the debt. (If it would take two pounds to buy what one used to buy, the national debt would be cut in half). The move destabilized all economic activity related to the pound, causing worldwide economic uncertainty.

2) The Smoot-Hawley tariff was passed, setting off a worldwide trade war. In the post–World War I era, America evolved into an increasingly isolationist community. The experience of active involvement in a European conflict, World War I, proved largely horrific. Most Americans wanted to withdraw from foreign conflicts and stay out. However, from an economic standpoint, World War I had opened the door to American exports on a full-scale basis. American goods stepped in to supply the necessities of life while all of Europe was focused on feeding the war machine. The American economy aggressively geared up to fill the exploding European demand. Sales of American goods were expanding exponentially, and the jobs required to support the sales growth were growing at a rapid rate. The booming economy of the 1920s seemed to support the notion that an isolated America could indeed survive on its own. However, many failed to understand that *in order to sustain the significant growth in the American economy, we had to continue the flow of exports.* The passage of the Smoot-Hawley tariff was a postwar reflection of Americans' desire to return to isolationism. The bill

placed excessive tariffs on nearly all manufactured imports. Politicians were confident that American-manufactured goods could fill the supply gap in foreign goods that would ensue. We needed to "buy American." Our leaders apparently did not expect any response from the Europeans. Retaliation did indeed take place as most European countries, in retaliation to Smoot-Hawley, enacted their own protective tariffs.

The new European tariffs were significant enough to virtually cut off most of America's exports. At the same time, the recovery of European agriculture after the World War virtually ended the need for American farm imports. Most US economists and politicians felt American-made goods could replace the European imports, most of which were priced out of the range of affordability by the excessive tariff. What was missed was the fact that many American-made goods were produced from parts imported from all over the globe. The significant increase in production costs led to a significant increase in the cost of everything made in America. The significant price increases led to an equally significant reduction in consumption. Hoover signed this tariff bill even though he had received a letter signed by more than one thousand economists warning him not to sign. A virtual trade war ensued, and the resulting cessation in the flow of exports and the significant increase in the cost of American-made goods helped push the country into a full-blown depression.

3) Congress increased the top personal income tax rate to 63 percent. Prior to our entry into World War

I, the income tax generated less than one-third of the federal revenue. Only a decade prior, wealthy business owners were allowed to retain most of their winnings and were free to reinvest in whatever way they deemed appropriate. Unburdened by the income tax, successful business owners were free to reinvest profits to expand their enterprises or establish new ventures. The imposition of a new significantly high tax on corporate profits and executive income virtually eliminated reinvestment. The wealthy began to hoard funds, asking why they should reinvest profits if the federal government was just going to take most of the increased earnings. Why invest in risky new ventures when the successful execution of the investment only resulted in higher taxes? The new tax rate sucked out funds that were sorely needed to grow the economy.

4) In response to all the economic uncertainty, the stock market crashed. Over the decade of the 1920s, the economic boom had everyone believing that the business of America was business. Americans believed in business and bought stocks at a frenetic pace (much of it on margin). The decade had seen the number of stockbrokers more than double. The working public followed the market with a passion it once reserved for baseball. Many plunged all their hard-earned savings into speculative stock, buying syndicates. Ninety percent of the stock purchased in the 1920s, by one estimate, was bought for speculation. Making matters worse, banks frequently accepted speculative stocks as collateral for margin loans. Many banks also had been among the most eager participants in the speculative

stock frenzy. In the soaring economy, banks had piled up large cash reserves. They invested these reserves heavily in the stock market, feeling it gave them the best opportunity for long-term growth. Suddenly the stock market crashed. With stocks down nearly 85 percent from their top, the banks found themselves with total assets worth less than they owed their depositors. They were holding collateral on a substantial portion of their loans in speculative stocks that were now worthless. Panic set in. Depositors began withdrawing funds, frequently demanding gold in lieu of paper money. Many banks would not survive. Between 1930 and 1932, 773 national banks and 3,604 state banks, with more than $2.7 billion in assets, had failed.

The global reaction to these four events destroyed the American economy. Given time, these issues likely would have been resolved. However, in 1932, 16 percent of the country was without work (remember there was no unemployment insurance), and there was no prospect for a quick turnaround. The electorate needed help, and those in desperate straits felt the federal government should help them. People everywhere were protesting. The free-enterprise economic system appeared to be failing. The economic opportunity that previously existed for every American was slipping away. Many politicians feared an armed revolt (after all, look at what was happening in Russia and Germany). Hoover stayed the course, and hope continued to fade.

The poor performance of the Federal Reserve during the initial entry into the Depression begs the question, what were they thinking? The Federal Reserve was created in 1913 to control the monetary system by regulating interest rates and by lending money to banks. The concept being that the Federal Reserve would set interest rates and lend funds to needy and worthy banks *with the intent of preventing bank failure*. Everyone knew that any significant volume of bank failures would lead to panic and a general banking collapse. In theory, throughout this period, the Fed should have been buying bonds in the open market to raise cash to lend to the struggling banking industry. What they did was raise interest rates four times from 3.5 percent to 6 percent during the period 1928–29. The higher interest rates made it harder for businesses to borrow money, adding another barrier to economic growth. The significant decline in general economic activity, which was partially a result of the higher borrowing rates, eventually led to meaningful stock market declines. When the stock market finally crashed, the Fed dithered, allowing panicked depositors to flood into the banks seeking to withdraw all their funds, most demanding to receive their withdrawal in the form of gold. The run on the banks led to the bank failures that were only halted by FDR's bank holiday. The Federal Reserve could have slowed or even prevented this crisis by lending money to the cash-hungry banks. Instead the Fed let the runs continue, allowing hundreds of significant banks to collapse into bankruptcy. The money, like unpaid loans, simply vanished. As banks failed, their assets disappeared. The inaction almost seems intentional. Is it possible that the Fed actually wanted to put a halt to the overexuberance of the 1920s?

The country entered a depression of unprecedented magnitude. Stocks had dropped over 85 percent, manufacturing had ground to a halt (the auto industry was operating at less than 20 percent capacity), and between one-quarter and one-third of the work force were unemployed. Many of those who actually held a job suffered with low wages and reduced work hours. Most people who actually found work were forced into sweatshop conditions with long hours and low wages. Soup kitchens handed out meager portions to millions of hungry people. Suffering was universal. Urban and rural Americans were united by the shared sense of desperation. In the farm belt, mobs were showing up at foreclosures, stopping the proceedings by force and sending the bank lawyers fleeing. In rural areas and small towns, talk of revolution was growing. Worst off were the residents of "Hooverville," sizable camps that were springing up in city parks and under bridges in nearly every American city. Hooverville residents slept in shacks pieced together with wood planks, cardboard, and tar paper, relying on meager scraps of food from the soup kitchens for nourishment. Many of the desperate were European immigrants who came to America with dreams of prosperity. The reality during the 1930s had become very frightening. Unschooled in the free-enterprise world, most were shocked at the apathy shown by the federal government. Correspondence from relatives that remained in the Old World let the immigrant know the political world was changing in Europe and Russia. The proletariat was on the rise. Old World governments were being forced to provide for the needy. When would America respond?

While the economy crumbled, President Hoover refused to take any aggressive steps to stem the tide. He believed the economic outlook would change once the excesses were "washed out" of the system. He firmly believed the fundamentals of the free-enterprise system would soon take over, balancing the supply and demand curves. Hoover understood that a reasonable period of suffering was necessary to clear the significant oversupply of goods and bring the economy back to normal. He believed that manufacturers and farmers simply needed time to adjust their production levels to compensate for the falling demand that came with the end of the war. Prosperity would return if everyone could just hold on a little longer.

The Democrats saw things differently. Their presidential candidate, Franklin D. Roosevelt was pledging to help the "forgotten man" while Hoover held tight to his Republican beliefs. Throughout the 1932 presidential campaign, Hoover declared that the campaign was not a contest between two men but one between two philosophies of government.

To a nation that was demanding government action, Hoover preached individualism. He stated that *it was not* the federal government's role to "relieve private institutions of their responsibility to the public or of local governments to the States, or of the States to the Federal government." Hoover wholeheartedly believed in laissez-faire economics. He had no plans to commit federal funds to problems he felt were best handled by local governments and private institutions.

Prior presidents resisted the temptation to provide federal funds for local aid packages. In 1887, several counties in Texas had faced a long drought, and many farmers lost their crops. Texas politicians pressed Congress to provide free seeds to the distressed farmers. The House and Senate passed bills to provide $10,000 in relief. President Grover Cleveland vetoed the bill, stating, "I can find no warrant for such appropriation in the Constitution." He added, "Federal aid in such cases encourages the expectations of paternal care on the part of the government and weakens the sturdiness of our national character."

Oddly enough, even FDR recognized the damage federal relief did to our national character. In the 1935 State of the Union address, he stated, "The lessons of history, confirmed by evidence immediately before me, show conclusively that continued dependence upon relief induces a spiritual and moral disintegration fundamentally destructive to the national fiber. To dole out relief in this way is to administer a narcotic, a subtle destroyer of the human spirit." His proposed solution was to provide "work relief." The switch from direct relief (FERA) to work relief (WPA) appeared to be an appropriate advance. However, many WPA projects were little more than make-work projects that accomplished little in the form of economic recovery. (See Obama's stimulus package to prove that history does repeat itself.)

In the1932 election campaign, FDR offered a clear alternative to Hoover. Early in the presidential campaign, in an April 7, 1932 radio address, he promised to champion "the forgotten man at the bottom of the economic pyramid." Roosevelt was promising direct federal help to those who lacked money or social status. In his nomination acceptance speech, he made a historic promise. "I pledge you, I pledge myself a new deal for the American people." His pledge of a new deal was a commitment to use the power of the federal government to bring about economic change, rather than wait for conditions to improve.

Roosevelt won in a landslide. March 4, 1933, his Inauguration Day, is the line in the sand that officially turned the tide against the free-enterprise economy.

He had surely received a public mandate for change. The public mandate was so soundly stated that all the initiatives proposed by the Roosevelt administration during the first hundred days received very little opposition from the Republicans in Congress. The laissez-faire free-enterprise platform of the Hoover campaign was soundly defeated. The election signaled a comprehensive change in the electorate. They demanded action, action *now*. And FDR was about to deliver. During his first hundred days in office, FDR used his electoral mandate to turn the country in a whole new direction, a giant leap into the age of entitlement.

A dejected Hoover, fully grasping the extent of the change that was about to take place, wrote after the election "That when the American people realize that they surrendered the freedom of mind and spirit for which their ancestors had fought and agonized for over 300 years, they will, I hope, recollect that I at least tried to save them."[11] Hoover could not overstate the extent of change that was about to occur. The age of rugged individualism and free enterprise ended with the election of Franklin Delano Roosevelt.

FDR's initial hundred days in office were the most intense period of lawmaking ever undertaken. Fifteen major bills passed, all with the intent of altering the relationship between the American government and the economy. In little more than three months, FDR invented a whole new America. One cannot overstate the revolutionary aspect of these changes. His hundred-day barrage of legislation laid the groundwork for today's overindulgent, overregulated society—the true beginning of the age of entitlement and the commencement of the American welfare state.

It all started with the Emergency Banking Act. Roosevelt took action to halt the run on the banks (that could have been prevented through aggressive action from the Fed) by declaring a bank holiday that closed the banks while the EBA legislation was pushed through. The emergency bill that was quickly passed saved the banking industry by allowing the Federal Reserve to issue notes used by the banks as currency

---

[11] Arthur M. Kovel Sr., *The Cycles of American History* (Boston: Houghton, Mifflin Company, 1986), 376–80.

(Federal Reserve notes). It also restricted the ability of the depositors to demand actual gold for their withdrawals. It was the first step in moving America away from the true gold/silver standard, as England had done earlier. Though only a stopgap measure, the Emergency Banking Act set the tone for the entire New Deal. Roosevelt threw aside Hoover's laissez-faire principals and made it clear that he considered it the federal government's duty to ensure the nation's economic institutions functioned properly. To meet that responsibility, FDR injected the federal government more deeply into private enterprise than it had ever gone before. Following the emergency action, Congress passed, and FDR signed, the Glass-Steagall Act. The bill included a number of reforms that had long been opposed by the Hoover administration. It raised capital requirements for new banks. It also provided that bank officers could be removed and imprisoned for up to five years for engaging in unsound practices, separated deposit banking from investment banking, and established the Federal Deposit Insurance Corporation (FDIC). All in all, this bill was an extensive and controversial governmental intrusion into the banking industry. FDR forced reform on the beleaguered bankers, following the lead of the last Democrat to hold the presidency, Woodrow Wilson.

Despite the radical move, some felt FDR had not gone far enough. Senator Bronson Cutting, a pro-Roosevelt Republican from New Mexico, wrote in *Liberty* magazine the following year, "The nationalization of banks by President Roosevelt could have been accomplished without a word or protest."[12] The fact that the statement was issued by a Republican is a great indicator of the mood of the nation

---

[12] The New Republic, 3/15/33.

at the time. One should recall that nationalization of the banking industry was attempted by President Wilson. He would have taken this approach without hesitation. America was in panic mode. Change was in the wind.

The desperation that prevailed had altered the outlook of most Americans. The free-enterprise-based laissez-faire approach to federal government that had existed for a century and a half had suddenly passed into history. Somehow the general population had come to believe that transferring control of nearly all aspects of the economy to the federal government was the solution to all the nation's woes. The impoverished masses had given up on the free-enterprise system, a system that had been a primary cornerstone of American freedom. As the economic situation worsened, many working within the government feared a revolution. (The Russian revolution was still fresh in their minds.) How long would the homeless, unemployed, desperate workers just sit back and take it? An environment where individuals lost their savings in bankrupt banks or were denied access to their funds could have been the spark that would start an armed insurrection. It would be unthinkable to deploy military forces to subdue American citizens if an insurrection occurred. FDR and his administration recognized the potential that the existing system was losing control of the masses. A newly devised system of federal economic management that delivered relief to those in need became their answer to control the masses.

After implementing the Emergency Banking Act, the next major triumph supporting the new economic management concept was the Agricultural Adjustment Act. FDR extended the special session of Congress so that this act could be voted upon. He had declared the Farm Act to be of equal importance to the banking crisis. The bill he said would be "a new and untrodden path." Indeed it was. Henry Wallace spearheaded the bill. It was drafted with the expectation of bringing the prices of seven basic commodities—wheat, cotton, hogs, beef, rice, tobacco, and milk—back up to prewar prices. It delegated broad powers to the president, so broad in fact that few could see their limits. The bill granted FDR the power to pay the farmer for taking land out of production. It financed the payment with a tax on processors (a tax that was later declared unconstitutional). It effectively gave the federal government control of the agricultural market.

Why take steps to cut back production when millions were starving? It is clear that they chose to attack the supply side of the economic curve primarily because it handed control of the marketplace over to the federal government. Had Roosevelt chosen to use government funds to purchase the oversupply, it likely would have cleared the market and restored the desired pricing levels in a much more effective fashion. It seems very strange that FDR and his administration elected to take millions of acres of food out of production and slaughtered millions of hogs when millions of Americans were going hungry. Why not purchase the oversupply and offer it to hungry Americans in exchange for their labor in public works projects? It would be a very worthwhile project to explore the act and the process involved in pushing it through Congress, as it represents the first successful federal effort to control an economic marketplace. Paying farmers not to work in exchange for government payments is our first forerunner of Freefare. Elements of this act remain in effect today.

Public works projects followed as a cornerstone of the FDR administrations plan for economic recovery. Secretary of Labor Francis Perkins was a strong proponent of the establishment of these public works plans. She believed that with jobs scarce, the government has a duty to provide work for the unemployed. She believed large-scale public works would prime the pump, creating economic activity that would eventually restore the economy. She and Harry Hopkins, a close advisor to FDR, pushed the president to start the projects. They pointed out that many progressives in Congress also believed that large-scale public works projects were the best hope for the immediate future. All believed that the majority of the unemployed did not want handouts; they wanted a paycheck. The private sector would not or could not produce the jobs needed. Perkins and Hopkins convinced FDR that the only method of creating the needed jobs was via public works projects. In the entire history of the federal government, there was no precedence to follow. FDR and his administration formulated the route and set us on the course, using the jobs provided as another element in the new federal economic management system.

Not all in the FDR administration were in favor. Lewis Douglas, Roosevelt's budget director, objected to the unfunded expense of such projects. Douglas feared the government would break under the sheer weight of interest and amortization of charges resulting from the cost of financing the projects with deficit funding. Douglas, an Arizona conservative, was alone in the FDR administration that was mostly filled with progressives. He lived in constant dread that "society was unraveling, that socialism was on the march, and that capitalism was in mortal danger." He was alarmed by what he called "these forces that are being released" and the "philosophical base upon which they rest."

He said he "had great apprehension for the future of my country."[13] How prophetic.

Despite Douglas's objections, the CCC (Civilian Conservation Corps) was launched and became the first in a number of public works projects initiated by the FDR administration. Reliance upon the federal government as a source of achieving desired levels of employment had its start, never to retreat. A meaningful element in emerging theory of controlling the masses by delivering benefits was firmly in place.

If Roosevelt was the leader of a new American revolution, the architects were the key members of his cabinet and his inner circle of advisors. These individuals became the creative conceptualists that developed the elements of a new federal control system being put in place to deliver multiple economic benefits to those in need—benefits used to subdue the angry masses.

Frances Perkins, secretary of labor, was the first woman ever to serve as a cabinet member. She became the leader of the progressive forces within the administration. As industrial commissioner in New York under Governor Roosevelt, she was a leading advocate for working men and women. Before accepting the cabinet position, she made Roosevelt promise to support federal relief, public works, minimum wage, maximum-hour laws, and a ban on child labor. By the end of the New Deal, her entire agenda had been enacted into law. She became the revolution's leading progressive influence, constantly pushing Roosevelt to enact her agenda. She had

---

[13] Letter of Lewis Douglas to W. R. Matthews on December 29, 1932, in Douglas Papers, Box 238; Letter of Lewis Douglas to Franklin Roosevelt in January 1922, in Douglas Papers, Box 238.

FDR's confidence, and she used her position to constantly promote one progressive initiative after another. Under her leadership, the free-enterprise system began to experience the first of many social constraints. Business was no longer free to operate at the discretion of the owner. Minimum wage and maximum hours were in place. No more child labor. Fair labor practices were now enforced by a federal bureaucracy. The working man had his advocate in place at a federal level.

Henry Wallace, son of an Iowa farmer/journalist, was the secretary of agriculture. As secretary of agriculture, he championed the Agricultural Adjustment Act (AAA). The AAA was the initial New Deal law committing the federal government to helping Depression victims. He managed the drafting of the act, aimed at propping up farm prices by having the federal government pay farmers to grow less (no work and pay a basic Freefare ideal). Though he personally hated the idea of reduced production, he conceded to the concept, as he felt other alternatives seemed far worse. The bill could have split the nation along rural and urban lines. However, the big-city representatives in Congress had long accepted that higher farm prices would make the farmer a better consumer, benefiting the nation as a whole. During the hundred-day commencement of the FDR administration, Wallace worked around the clock to obtain passage of the AAA. There was a clear need to put farm constraints in place before the spring crops were planted. There were many heated debates in Congress over the controversial legislation. Finally, riding FDR's electoral mandate, Wallace prevailed, and Congress approved the legislation. On May 12, 1932, FDR signed the Agricultural Adjustment Act into law, and the economics of American agriculture was permanently changed. Although it got off to a slow start, the AAA had a dramatic impact on the prices of wheat, cotton, corn, and hogs. Federal control of the marketplace worked. The AAA eliminated agricultural oversupply, and by 1936 farm income had increased by 50 percent. The biggest problem with the New Deal farm programs administered by Wallace was that once in place, they proved impossible to eliminate. Government intrusion into the free-enterprise farming marketplace was supposed to be temporary. The AAA was designed to end when the national economic emergency in agriculture was over. The agricultural emergency ended when the Depression did, but the farm programs never went away. When Wallace stepped down as secretary of agriculture to run as Roosevelt's second-term vice president, he left behind a department that had grown from 40,000 employees when he took office to one that employed more than 146,000. In only four years, he successfully set a precedent for the future—the development of unrelenting growth of the federal bureaucracy to support the ever-increasing federal control of everything.

Rexford Tugwell served as one of FDR's closest advisors. The young economist, born in Upstate New York, was teaching at Columbia when he was recruited to the administration by Raymond Moley. FDR was no economist; in fact, he had little or no economic aptitude. He desperately needed someone to guide him on economic issues. Tugwell filled the bill. Moley, who had headed FDR's brain trust during the presidential campaign, recommended Tugwell, having been a colleague of his at Columbia. Moley had great respect for Tugwell's intellect and charm. FDR easily accepted him to the team.

Tugwell believed that government, industry, and agriculture should work together—a concept he branded "concert of interests." Tugwell's deep knowledge of the economics of agriculture neatly complemented Henry Wallace's practical experience. As a much-published economic theorist, Tugwell thought about agriculture in ways Wallace had not. In 1927, he had traveled to the Soviet Union with a trade union delegation and had seen collective planning up close. He returned with ideas about how American agriculture could be improved through greater government intervention. He then enthusiastically worked in concert with Wallace, drafting and passing the Agricultural Adjustment Act. He remained as a trusted advisor to Roosevelt and functioned as the administration's strongest proponent of government involvement in every aspect of the economy. The journalist Ernest K. Lindley regarded Tugwell as "the philosopher, the sociologist and the prophet of the Roosevelt Revolution, as well as one of its boldest practitioners."[14] Tugwell served as the primary source of economic strategy. He was a progressive with strong socialist leaning. He, more than any other, championed the movement to socialize economic activity.

Harry Hopkins only entered the FDR administration for the last twenty-one of the first one hundred days (but he continued to serve for the majority of the remaining four terms). He quickly made up for lost time. As administrator of the Federal Emergency Relief Act, he put together one of the most dynamic, innovative departments in the federal government. FERA established for the first time the principle that providing food, clothing, and other necessities was a federal responsibility, something previously left to states, localities, and local charities. Hopkins used the legislation to create a social welfare system that operated on a single set

---

[14] Ernest K Lindley, Roosevelt Revolution, Viking Press, New York, pp 304-07

of national standards. Once his relief system was in place, Hopkins pushed to create public works jobs—real jobs, not just make-work projects assigned to work off the welfare benefits. He persuaded FDR to let him start a new public works program focused on smaller programs that could be started quickly, the Civil Works Administration (CWA). Hopkins immediately transferred the FERA work relief recipients into the CWA. He also began hiring thousands of unemployed into the program. Hopkins spent with abandon. He quickly had more than 810,000 people on the payroll. The 200,000 projects completed by the CWA ranged from tearing down dilapidated houses to extending municipal sewer systems. His workers rebuilt schools, built playgrounds and swimming pools, and engaged in malaria control and tick eradication. The CWA was short-lived, but it was the biggest public works program that ever existed in America. It turned the New Deal's focus even more toward providing the unemployed with jobs. Later, in 1934, Hopkins lobbied Roosevelt to create more public works. Roosevelt agreed to a new $4.8 billion program (remember Hoover ran the entire federal government on $4 billion), the Works Progress Administration (WPA). Hopkins essentially ran the program. In its lifetime, the WPA employed 8.5 million people and supported 20 million, more than 20 percent of the population. Hopkins would go on to become FDR closest advisor, his alter ego. Francis Perkins stated that Hopkins was "truly another self for President Roosevelt." She went on to state, "The mutual trust between the two men sprang, of course, from personal sympathy and temperamental harmony, but more from a common devotion to the idea that their mission in life was to make things better for the people."

Hopkins went on to fill a number of critical positions in the FDR administration. His wartime service was historic. However, his leadership of FERA, CWA, and the WPA was his most enduring legacy. The relief and public works programs he set in motion were as important as any part of the New Deal in changing the relationship between the federal government and its citizens.

How on earth were all of these initiatives financed? Taxes were part of the answer. In an effort to generate the needed cash, FDR launched an assault on the wealthy. He pushed hard for increases in the top tax rate for those in the upper-income brackets. At one point, he actually asked Congress to pass a 100 percent tax on all earned income in excess of $100,000! He also used the audit power of the IRS to target wealthy individuals he felt were avoiding their fair share. He relentlessly pressed for increased taxes on undistributed corporate taxes. Even though he himself was from a wealthy family, his keen political sense recognized the distain the voting public felt toward those who were well off. He literally waged war on the upper class. However, he did not limit his efforts to the wealthy. Roosevelt embraced the excise tax, imposing it on more things than any previous president. Historically, the excise tax was a fee charged on so-called vices, starting with the whiskey tax in 1790s. What better way to raise government funds than through an attack on individual vices? Most economists consider excise taxes regressive because they hit lower-income groups proportionally more heavily than the wealthier groups. This was especially true with FDR. Before the Depression, most excise taxes were generated from taxes on tobacco and alcohol. In 1932, President Hoover, with the support of Democrat congressmen, introduced a host of new duties as a one-year emergency measure (sounds like Wilson's "temporary" income tax to cover the cost of WWI) to offset revenues lost during the Depression. Duties were placed on cars, movie tickets, radios, long-distance telephone calls, stock transfers, yachts, furs, and a new excise tax of one cent tax on gasoline. To demonstrate the scope of these new taxes, it is interesting to note that once these taxes went into effect, they became the first federal taxes that most Americans paid. (The income tax with its high personal exemptions only covered the top 3 percent of Americans). Roosevelt chose to retain Hoover's *emergency* excises once he realized how painlessly he could collect taxes from all classes of consumers (after all, it was easy for them to just consider it part of the price). By 1935, the federal excise tax revenue exceeded $1.36 billion while income tax revenue was only $527 million. Clearly FDR not only retained the excise taxes; he expanded the categories and increased the percentages. To avoid drawing attention to these taxes, he said very little about them publically. However, in a budget message of January 5, 1939, he summarized his support for continuing the taxes. In a message to Congress, he made a statement that would be fully embraced by future politicians. He outlined his support "not because I regard them as ideal components of our tax structure, but because their collection has been perfected, our economy is adjusted to them, and we cannot afford at this time to sacrifice the revenue they represent."[15]

Even with the significant expansion of the excise tax, FDR was substantially outspending the revenues. How then did he fill the gap? Enter the national debt! The United States had budget surpluses in 1930 and 1931. With the onslaught of federal assistance, it did not take FDR long to substantially

---

[15] "Statements on Taxes by Members of This Administration in 1939" in Morgenthau Diary, January 1939.

outspend the skyrocketing federal income. When FDR took office in 1931, the national debt stood at $16 billion (keep in mind that Hoover ran the entire federal government in 1930 with a budget of $4 billion and achieved a surplus). By the end of the decade, that debt grew to over $40 billion. In less than a decade, the national debt grew ten times more than it had in the previous 150 years of our country's existence!

The first hundred days of the FDR administration became a moral revolution. The entire philosophy regarding the role of the federal government in the American economic process changed forever. The bills passed and the institutions created were not nearly as significant as the philosophical change they represent. The overall mind-set of those in power had changed from laissez-faire, hands-off, to a duty to provide security, oversight, and control. Oversight of financial institutions and control of the general marketplace were justified as a means to end the ignorance, greed, and apathy that had emerged under the Republican administrations in the 1920s. Private enterprise could no longer be trusted to do what was right for the average American. The greedy businessman needed to be controlled, and the public needed protection.

Federal oversight of private institutions and the assumption of control over most of the private enterprise marketplace marked a significant philosophical change in the role of the federal government. The American free-enterprise experiment was essentially over once this change in philosophy was combined, with the expectation that the federal government would provide jobs and family security whenever the private sector faltered. In a little over three months, capitalism was mortally wounded, and socialism was indeed on the march.

Pushing the philosophical departure established in the first hundred days, the country's new "benevolent dictator," FDR, moved on to the New Deal, part 2. He continued to search for ways to expand federal power over economic activities in support of his new theory to control the masses. He and his brain trust initiated a number of economic initiatives that would have made Karl Marx proud. Roosevelt was on a mission to control every aspect of the economy. He created the National Industrial Recovery Act (NRA), developed to control prices and wages. NRA oversight panels were appointed to determine proper production levels, hours worked, and wages paid by industry group and publish those standards in an industry NRA code. Violators not conforming to the code actually faced fines and prison time. Public pressure was applied to every business to conform to the codes developed on an industry by industry basis. Those in compliance displayed the famous blue eagle sign, assuring the public they were in compliance with the code. Few were willing to resist, and no one seemed to draw comparisons to the tactics being used in Stalin's Soviet Union. After two years of massive efforts to promote the act by Roosevelt and thousands of hours of work writing millions of detail into 546 codes, the Supreme Court found the program so patently unconstitutional not one of the nine justices would condone it. FDR's response was to initiate an aggressive attempt to stack the court with justices that would condone his assault on the Constitution. He spent nearly all of his political capital attempting to convince Congress to support his assault on the Supreme Court. The high court seemed to be standing in the way of his plan to fix America.

Despite the series of Supreme Court setbacks, the scope and size of the federal government was expanding exponentially. George McJimsey, who wrote the FDR issue of the distinguished American Presidency Series, concludes, "One of Roosevelt's major achievements was to create an institutional structure for the modern welfare state. Subsequent Presidents were freer than ever to use government in creative ways."

FDR was firmly committed to rearranging American economic life permanently. "Centralize power," he argued, and "reduce the influence of free choice to create new economic arrangements between employee and employer." The primary tools he sought to engage were minimum-wage laws (or "wages and hours laws," as he termed it) and social security.

Frances Perkins, the secretary of labor, was the administration's strongest advocate for labor law reform. She made it her mission from the very beginning of the administration to convince FDR to support a minimum-wage and maximum-hour law along with a restriction on child labor. They first had success by including minimum-wage sections built into the NRA codes. When the NRA was struck down by the Supreme Court in 1935, Roosevelt began promoting a minimum-wage law. Many congressmen opposed it for constitutional reasons. Others feared the law would increase unemployment. An alliance of New England Democrats and Republicans, however, came to FDR's support. The driving force behind the New England coalition was their desire to support their textile industry. During the late 1920s, the American textile industry had begun a shift from New England to the South, where the cost of living was lower and where southern workers produced a high-quality product for lower wages. Politicians from Massachusetts, led by Republican Senator Henry Cabot Lodge Jr., battled in Congress for the minimum-wage law that would force the southern textile mills to raise their wages and lose their competitive edge. Southern congressmen fought valiantly against the bill. Their opposition was effective in the 1937 Congress, and they were actually successful in handing FDR his first setback in New Deal legislation when the proposed law failed to pass. However, Lodge, with FDR's full political support, finally won out in 1938 with the passage of the Fair Labor Standards Act. The law set the minimum wage at twenty-five cents an hour, with additional provisions to increase it to forty cents an hour over the next seven years.

The Fair Labor Standards Act of 1938 represents a monumental shift in the economic landscape of America. With the passage of this law, the federal government inserted itself as a party to every agreement made between every American employer and employee. It established the federal bureaucracy as a policing force to assure fairness in the employer/employee relationship. FDR successfully injected a measure of federal control over a key segment of the free-enterprise economy; the freedom to build a labor force at a labor rate offered and accepted by a willing worker was now subject to federal constraints. The new law represented a formidable beachhead in the FDR administration's war on free enterprise. Once one concedes the right of the federal government to establish a *fair* minimum wage and *reasonable* maximum hours worked, how far away are we from allowing them to declare a *fair* maximum wage and conceding the ability to ration hours worked? The Fair Labor Standards Act established precedence for future federal laws that would impose even greater controls on the American businessman and the American economy.

FDR also endorsed legislation that once successfully established would most significantly affect future generations—social security.

The initial proposal for a federal retirement plan was outlined by a California physician, Francis Townsend, who stirred supports throughout the country for his plan to have the federal government give $200 per month to all retirees over age sixty (sounds like a Freefare advocate). FDR rejected the concept but quickly developed his own federal retirement plan. In his plan, employees paid a maximum of thirty dollars per year (1 percent on each dollar of earned income up to $3,000) into a mandatory retirement plan. Employers had to match the payment and send it all to Washington. At age sixty-two, the employee would be eligible to receive $22.54 per month in retirement benefits (not bad—put in $60 per year, take out $270.48 per year). The mandatory program began in 1937 with the first payout beginning in 1940 (giving the initial deposits for 1940 retirees three years to grow 450 percent, he obviously was aware that substantial federal subsidy would be needed for the initial recipients).

The contribution percentages and the payout amounts were subject to change by Congress. Once the plan was initiated, an accountant quizzed Roosevelt about the economics of the program. Roosevelt's response was, "I guess you are right about the economics, but those taxes were never a problem of economics. They are politics all the way through. With those taxes in there no damn politician will ever scrap my social security program."[16] How astute. The establishment of social security firmly entrenched the federal bureaucracy in the financial management of every family in America. The American worker somehow accepted the intrusion, complying with the mandates with barely

---

[16] Frank Fridel, *Franklin D. Roosevelt: A Rendezvous with Destiny* (Boston: Little, Brown, 1990), 150.

a whimper. After all, it was only 1 percent, thirty dollars per year, and it was something everyone should be doing anyway. We give up thirty dollars per year, and now the government will care for us when we grow old. Following implementation of social security, most politicians delighted in raising social security payouts and using the increases to garner votes from the elderly. The political mind never seems to grasp the long-term financial consequences of retirement benefits. Few even attempted to calculate the financial dilemma that FDR created. Decade after decade, liberal politicians continued to enhance the program with little or no regard to the funding that would be required once the volume of retirees began to multiply.

During the original debate in the Senate on social security, Senator Bennett Champ Clark of Missouri wondered if private pensions for retirement might outperform the government pensions proposed in the social security bill. He introduced the Clark Amendment, which would have allowed private employers to opt out of social security with the proviso that they would at least match the government program and would place the premiums with an insurance company or approved alternative. Given that many private pension plans over the past sixty years have returned around 8 percent per year and social security benefits have averaged less than 2 percent, Senator Clark's concerns were well founded. Roosevelt clearly stated that this bill was not about economics. It was all about politics. The social security legislation served to establish *permanent* control over a substantial segment of the population and *permanently embed* an administrative bureaucracy. Many of the New Deal programs were viewed as temporary relief efforts designed to spurn on the economy. Roosevelt leveraged the popularity of these temporary relief programs to push through a program he knew would become a prominent American institution.

From 1937 to 1940, the federal treasury held the social security funds in an earmarked account. After the early 1940s, it became a pay-as-you-go program when the federal government usurped the unused funds. Roosevelt was a very astute politician and a very committed socialist. The social security plan established a permanent foundation on which future liberals could construct the modern welfare state. Forcing every employee and their employer to send monthly tithes to the federal government for a promise to pay future retirement benefits was an amazing accomplishment, a giant step toward socialism.

A primary cornerstone of all socialist governments lies in the guarantee of a standard of living after retirement. Universal submission to the concept of mandatory funding for retirement income financed through mandated contributions by both the employee and the employer with all funds being held by the federal government represented a monumental step away from a free-enterprise economy. Encouragement of private investment in individual retirement accounts supported with employer contributions would have been a more appropriate free-enterprise approach to this issue. FDR was not about to use the free-enterprise approach, as it failed to impose the level of control he was seeking. If one controls the funds, one is capable of controlling the individual. Comply with the control or lose the funds!

The psychological impact of the Social Security Act on America's workers was enormous. If the progressive acts pushed through Congress during the first hundred days act as the foundation of the modern welfare state, the Social Security Act is the framework to which all future programs attach. Once social security was established, the American worker was permanently enlisted in the federal establishment and forever forfeited most of the economic freedoms that earlier generations fought so hard to protect. The Russian revolution and the rise of Fascism in Germany were militaristic and bloody. The Roosevelt administration sent us down a similar path without firing a shot or drawing a drop of blood. How this did happen and why was it so easy?

Prior to the passage of the social security legislation in 1937, the concept of retirement funding for the working class was virtually nonexistent. In today's world of 401Ks IRAs, and pension plans, it is hard to conceive of entering retirement without a funded retirement plan to supplement social security. To FDR's credit, he recognized the lack of retirement planning and recognized the benefit of mandating the creation of retirement plans. However, being the ever-resourceful politician with a clear agenda to establish federal control, he also recognized a unique opportunity to commandeer funds and establish a new bureaucracy that could substantially enhance his socialist agenda. Importing all funding into the federal bureaucracy guaranteed continued federal control. Once funds were flowing, no politician would ever garnish the support to end the program or privatize it.

The psychological impact on the initial generations participating in the social security program is worthy of further study. Embracing the concept that a worker could give the federal government thirty dollars a year with the understanding that they would be taken care of in retirement caused most workers of the time to feel comfortable spending all they made. There was no need to put aside any more funds for retirement. Social security was in place, and most considered that the social security funds would be all that was needed to fund their retirement. Employers took the same approach. They pointed to their employer match as the method they considered fulfillment of any retirement obligation they held for employees. It would take several decades for the participants to realize that the retirement funds coming from social security would provide only a small portion of the funding needed to finance retirement. By then, for most, it was too late. The inadequacy that should have been easily predictable from the outset would become even clearer once Congress usurped the funding and made the program a pay-as-you-go system in the early 1940s. Most today would consider this pay-as-you-go approach to be the world's biggest Ponzi scheme. It will only survive with a growing base of participants paying greater and greater funds to the initial investors who are withdrawing significantly more funds than they put in. Increased life expectancy continues to add to the deficit. FDR and his economists were very aware of the inadequacies. The earlier quote cited above indicates he was aware the economics of the program were flawed. His response was, "It was not about the economics but about politics through and through." How unfortunate for those of us living in the twenty-first century.

All the initiatives instituted by FDR in the 1930s failed to motivate an economic recovery. Despite all the federal programs and federal stimulus spending, the economy in 1939 was equally as bad as it was in 1932. Unemployment remained at or near 20 percent. Employment growth was constrained by financial drain caused by the minimum wage and social security legislation. Farm subsidies failed to fully achieve the intended long-term results as many farmers, forsaking the subsidy, produced more output from reduced acreage by using better fertilizers and more efficient technologies.

It is likely that many of FDR's programs would have been amended or discarded had the New Deal not be saved by the Second World War. Focus on the war, accompanied by the skyrocketing demand for goods to support the war effort, turned attention away from the economic failure of the New Deal. The leadership provided in the war effort revived FDR's failing political life. The average American embraced the war leadership image he projected. Few could conceive America without him at the helm.

The fact that FDR passed away while in office after successfully leading America to victory in the Second World War became the final act that cemented his legacy. Any potential to revoke the New Deal passed away with him.

In his decade and a half of leadership, he had truly reinvented America. His administration ended a century and a half of carefully crafted free-enterprise precedence that had minimized the role of the federal government. His New Deal totally repositioned America.

The federal bureaucracy would henceforth be the primary controlling force in the life of every American.

CHAPTER 7

Lyndon Johnson's Great Society

The presidents following FDR (Truman and Eisenhower) focused on postwar recovery and did very little to enhance or diminish the New Deal. The recovered economy and the dramatic changes in attitude, confidence, and national pride resulting from the successful war efforts virtually eliminated the need for more social subsidies. The economy found its footing, and the desperation that drove the New Deal disappeared. For two full decades, Americans were back on their feet, relishing their roles as participants in the world's dominant economy. The economic catastrophe that was the driving force for the New Deal was becoming a distant memory, something that aging parents and grandparents referred to in apocalyptic terms while their children and grandchildren were flourishing in an economic wonderland that may never be seen again. The war had broken the New Deal's drive toward a fully managed economy, and Truman and Eisenhower were perfectly happy to leave things alone and just stand back and let the economic engine churn.

With the turn of the decade that had brought us Elvis and television came the 1960 presidential election. A youthful, fresh-faced war hero, John Kennedy, campaigned against the establishment's candidate, Richard Nixon. Kennedy was an appealing candidate, but he faced an uphill battle against Eisenhower's vice president. The polls were close. In an effort to bring the southern democrats into his camp, Kennedy selected Lyndon Johnson as his vice president. Johnson, a well-respected member of Congress, hailed from Texas and added a geographic balance to the Democratic ticket headed by the former Massachusetts senator, Kennedy. Little thought was given to the prospect that the New Deal Democrat from Texas could ascend to the Presidency. Fate has a way of working its magic.

Kennedy won in one of the closest elections in history. His inaugural speech gave us a clear indication of how he felt about more federal programs and more federal control. His quote, "ask not what your country can do for you, ask what you can do for your country" became one of the most quoted phrases of the era. Kennedy understood that the president's role was to continue to motivate economic opportunity. Opportunity for everyone to find employment, participate in economic growth, and contribute to society.

JFK surely intended to stem the entitlement tide. His vision was to serve as a leader committed to engendering self-reliance and self-fulfillment. He brought new energy and a fresh outlook to the White House. Kennedy recognized the need to create sustainable economic opportunity for all the emerging baby boomers regardless of race or color. Initiatives like the Peace Corps and the space program enhanced our international image and built confidence. JFK brought a youthful enthusiasm focused on building a better America.

His vision for the Civil Rights movement was to assure equal opportunity gained through integrated education, hiring quotas, and equal access to services. Believing the way out of multigenerational poverty was best achieved through economic empowerment, the initiatives he proposed, unlike FDR, were not centered on federal giveaway programs and welfare.

Suddenly, in November 1963, all the euphoria ended. Shots fired from the Texas School Book Depository in Dallas ended the dream. Kennedy was assassinated, and the well-established New Deal Democrat, Lyndon Johnson ascended to the presidency. Fate brought America a new president completely devoted to the FDR concept of controlling the masses by delivering benefits.

In 1931 Lyndon stepped off the train that had brought him from his hometown of Johnson City, Texas, and he soaked in his first taste of the political center of the world, Washington, DC. His positive political activities in Johnson City had gained the attention of Congressman Richard Kleberg from the Fourteenth Congressional District. Kleberg had an opening for a new legislative assistant. He selected JBJ. Johnson arrived in Washington just in time to be caught up in the New Deal euphoria. The challenges he had faced growing up in an economically challenged household made LBJ an easy convert. He fully embraced the New Deal and FDR leadership. He labored tirelessly in support of both.

He was fortunate to enter Washington just as the political universe was evolving from a decade of conservative Republican leadership to the progressive/liberal New Deal, a transition that coincided with his personal outlook. The timing of his arrival offered a unique opportunity to observe and participate in the transition firsthand. Lyndon made the most of the opportunity. He used his position as Kleberg's legislative assistant to successfully lobby for appointment as the Texas director of FDR's National Youth Administration. He then used that position to gain enough local notoriety to campaign for a seat in Congress that had become available when James Buchanan from Brenham, Texas, passed away. Johnson managed to win in a special runoff election. He became a congressman at age twenty-nine. His key to victory was his staunch support of FDR and the New Deal. He was the only local candidate to endorse FDR's proposal to enlarge the Supreme Court to fifteen members in order to ensure a pro-New Deal majority.

There can be little doubt about LBJ's personal views. He fully embraced the concept that the federal government owed a minimum standard of living to every American resident. He was determined to limit the wealth and power of the growing population of wealthy business executives. Politics limited what he could publically state, but his aggressive pursuit of the Great Society was a clear reflection of his progressive DNA. Much later in life (after his presidency), Johnson stated the following:

> When I thought about what type of Congressman I wanted to be I thought about my Populist grandfather and promised myself that I would always be the people's Congressman, representing all the people, not just the ones with money and power.
>
> My grandfather taught me early in life that neither misery nor squalor is inevitable so long as the government and the people are one … so long as the government assumes the positive role of eliminating the special interests that cause most of the problems in America—particularly the moneylenders largely confined in New York, Chicago and Boston. They'd always

been paid proportionately a far higher percentage of the total end product than they deserved. They lived off our sweat, and even before air conditioning they didn't know what sweat was. They just clipped coupons and wrote down debentures we couldn't spell and stole our pants out from under us. And because of them {the moneylenders} the guy who produces that tall piece of maize over there—pointing to a field hand—never gets what he deserves. They are leeches, cancerous, and they'd be unnecessary evils if we ever had the right kind of money management. And they control our banking and money system. If we ever have a revolution and throw out our system for Communism or Fascism, they will be the prime reason for it and the first victim. I believed it as a child and I believe it still.[17]

The quote clearly demonstrates the foundation for LBJ's pursuit of the Great Society. One should have no doubt that Lyndon Johnson was through and through a New Deal Democrat. Though it took nearly two decades to transition from FDR to LBJ, Johnson would waste no time pressing his version of the New Deal, the Great Society, once he gained the presidency.

Unlike Kennedy, Johnson firmly believed in federal assistance over self-reliance. He believed that everyone in

---

[17] *Lyndon Johnson and the American Dream*, Doris Kearns Goodwin, page 91.

America should not only be guaranteed an equal chance at success but also be insured against the possibility of total defeat. Johnson wanted to give his people everything this principal suggested, and he wanted them to have it at once. So the agenda was established; the Great Society would offer something to almost everyone—Medicare for the old, educational assistance for the young, tax rebates for business, higher minimum wage for labor, subsidies for farmers, vocational training for the unskilled, food for the hungry, housing for the homeless, poverty grants for the poor, clean highways for commuters, legal protection for the blacks, improved schooling for the Indians, rehabilitation for the lame, higher benefits for the unemployed, reduced quotas for immigration, auto safety for drivers, pensions for the retied, fair labeling for consumers, conservation for hikers and campers, and more and more and more. None of his fellow citizens' desires were wholly beyond his ability to satisfy.[18]

Johnson seemed to regard the programs of the Great Society in the way overly fond parents look at their children. By building on the strengths of prosperity rather than on the necessities of depression, the program of the Great Society would fulfill all the hopes that had been beyond the reach of the New Deal. It would accomplish more for the nation than had the programs of any other administration.[19]

Johnson was truly motivated by a desire to improve the lot of the disenfranchised. He had personally witnessed the Great Depression and experienced the misery that comes

---

[18] *Lyndon Johnson and the American Dream*, Doris Kearns Goodwin, page 216.

[19] *Lyndon Johnson and the American Dream*, Doris Kearns Goodwin, page 219.

with living in abject poverty. He was an FDR protégé and a faithful New Dealer. FDR had clearly demonstrated the political skill to mold the nation to his desire. LBJ took note and set about implementing his legislation with even greater skill than FDR. He saw a wealthy, prosperous nation and understood that with his 1964 electoral mandate he could leverage his popularity and forge the legislation that would create his Great Society.

The enormous volume of Johnson's social welfare programs served to permanently establish the age of entitlement. His desire to take care of his people motivated an endless barrage of legislative initiatives intended to guarantee a minimum standard of living to all Americans. Gradually the legislation created its own momentum. If we pass legislation to take care of one needy class, how can we ignore the others? Within the Great Society, the mission became that everyone in need should be taken care of. Program after program was legislated into existence with the intent of accomplishing this goal. The economy was strong, and the tax increases imposed to support the legislation felt like a meaningful contribution to society. The broad spectrum of programs forming the basis of Johnson's Great Society generated an even greater layer of federal bureaucracy than the New Deal. Thousands of additional employees were needed to perform all the administrative functions supporting the federal benefits. More bureaucracy, more control, more spending, more taxes!

The most impactful of all the legislation was Medicare. Johnson promoted the legislation designed to provide access to affordable medical coverage to America's elderly. Health care insurance premiums in the private marketplace were becoming prohibitive. More and more elderly Americans were dropping their coverage and entering retirement without medical insurance. With life expectancy expanding and the population of retirees increasing, the number of elderly uninsured was reaching crises levels. More and more uninsured elderly Americans were losing their retirement nest egg to hospital stays and medical care. LBJ was determined to fix the situation. His solution, Medicare, seemed simple. Provide federally subsidized affordable insurance coverage to the elderly. Premiums would be affordable (under fifty dollars per month) and would be deductible directly from social security payment (thus avoiding collection/cancellation problems). The insurance would contain reasonable deductibles and would cover both hospital stays and doctor bills. Costs could be contained by controlling reimbursement levels associated with all medical treatments—a federally administered cost containment program. More bureaucracy, more control. Federal payments to doctors and hospitals came with the proviso that the Medicare system would only reimburse a fair and equitable amount. Medicare established a new system of cost analysis to determine appropriate reimbursement levels. Providing care to Medicare patients was mandated, and doctors, hospitals, and all medical care givers were required to accept Medicare reimbursement regardless of the actual cost of the services provided.

The psychological impact of Medicare on the standard of living expectations of all who have retired or are planning retirement is enormous. Paired with social security, Medicare serves to guarantee a meaningful standard of living for all American elderly. American workers needed only to reach the finish line, set at age sixty-five, enroll in Social Security and Medicare, and they could live comfortably thereafter. For three decades, social security seemed to eliminate the need for retirement savings. The new Medicare program would allow maturing Americans the freedom to ignore the need to save for, or negotiate for, retirement medical insurance. Private-sector competition that may have generated an affordable solution for those who were retiring was eliminated, as the federal program applied to everyone and was mandatory. FDR had indicated that social security was not about the math; it was political through and through. The same could be said about LBJ's Medicare plan. None of the politicians cared to calculate the actual long-term cost of the program. It was good politics, and if the money was short, it could be hidden on the form of another tax on something nobody would notice. It was all about satisfying the political constituency, enlisting a loyal following, and garnering votes.

Anyone with even a slight math aptitude should be able to understand that the Medicare math could never work. The private market cost for health insurance covering the elderly accurately reflected the cost of the increased frequency and severity of medical issues that naturally come as part of the aging process. Medicare covers the highest-risk population of subscribers in the country for a premium of less than one hundred dollars per month per subscriber. The private market provider premiums would easily exceed $600 per month. The nominal premiums paid by the Medicare subscribers actually cover only a minor percentage of the covered Medicare expenses. Substantial subsidies are required to fill the shortfall. Skyrocketing medical inflation fueled by increased utilization and significant advancements in medical technology have combined with an increasing life expectancy and a growing population of elderly Americans to make Medicare a financially unsustainable program. Fearing the political ramification that would come from altering the program, the only solutions our esteemed politicians embrace is to increase current tax levels and invent and impose new hidden taxes. Each tax removes more and more cash from the economy and acts as a meaningful constraint on America's economic ability to compete and grow. Every congressman will admit that long-term financing problems exist with Medicare, yet each sitting Congress has only pushed the problem down the road. A significant financial crisis looms on the horizon.

Johnson's Great Society became the third stage in the socialist evolution that will eventually lead us to Freefare. Woodrow Wilson did the groundwork, establishing the income tax as the primary means of wealth redistribution. The New Deal then permanently changed the direction of the country and set the foundation for the modern welfare State. FDR's second revolution abandoned federal laissez-faire and changed our free enterprise economic system to a limited enterprise system, creating a huge federal bureaucracy and permanently cementing it with social security. LBJ then built the second story with his Great Society. His Great Society permanently embedded a national entitlement mentality. The Medicare and Medicaid programs working hand in hand with social security guaranteed there would be no turning back.

The age of entitlement was at hand.

CHAPTER 8

The Carter Administration

This will be a short chapter, about as short as the Ford and Carter administrations. The post-Nixon American voter of the late 1960s was totally fed up with politicians and the political process. They rejected Gerald Ford—Nixon's fill-in, a long-term Washington insider, and elected a total Washington outsider, Jimmy Carter.

Carter ascended to the presidency with very little experience dealing with national and international issues. This shortfall left him totally unprepared to wrestle with the bureaucratic monster that the New Deal and Great Society had created. The economy he inherited was beginning to buckle under the weight of the maturing social welfare obligations. The weak economy and the skyrocketing social welfare financial obligations doomed his administration to failure.

Unemployment was stubbornly high, and inflation was out of control. Carter and his economic advisors were totally unequipped to deal with the complexity of this two-headed monster. They were facing an economic catch-22. If they resolved the unemployment issue, it would fuel even greater inflation. On the other hand, the only way to restrain the inflation, they believed, was to tolerate (or even encourage) a high unemployment rate.

During this same time frame, more and more Americans were reaching age sixty-five, the magic age at which elderly Americans would become eligible to cash in on the promise of social security and Medicare, the lasting legacies of the New Deal and the Great Society. The post-Nixon budget makers annually grappled with funding, realizing that the math associated with these two programs simply did not work. The Washington insiders knew how to juggle the books to present the illusion of adequate financing. How could anyone expect a Washington outsider possessing only limited experience in running the state of Georgia to possess the knowledge and ability to conceive a politically acceptable method of stabilizing the economy and resolving the financial shortfalls of the maturing social security program? Failure was inevitable.

The retirement of the Depression-era population, the initial recipients of FDR's social security program, commenced in earnest in the early 1970s. Inflation-adjusted benefits were streaming out of Washington to the recipients at a pace that dwarfed their individual contributions. Retirees whose initial contributions to the program were well under one hundred dollars a month began receiving several hundred dollars a month in benefits. Funding initially intended to be maintained in a social security trust fund had been quickly amended to flow into the general funds, becoming part of the annual federal budget process. The outflow to the recipients was now placing severe strain on the general budget. The politically acceptable response to the expected cash shortfall was to supply funding through increasing taxes and borrowing more funds, adding to an ever-growing national debt.

During this same period, LBJ's Medicare program was becoming the exclusive means of covering the medical obligations of those over age sixty-five. Soaring medical inflation, partially fueled by the increased utilization of the Medicare recipients, exerted additional strain on the budget. The national debt was mounting, and the long-term outlook appeared bleak. The post–World War II baby boomer generation was maturing. Social security and Medicare, having been in existence for several decades, had become expected entitlements all baby boomers believed they had earned. The math to finance future baby boomer entitlement benefits had not improved. Actuaries began pointing to increasing life expectancy and ever-increasing medical inflation to support their projection of pending disaster. Unadjusted, it was becoming evident that these two social welfare programs had the potential to bankrupt America.

So how could an inexperienced Washington outsider possess the political capital to amend these well-entrenched entitlements? It wasn't going to happen.

The social welfare entitlement programs present a substantial dilemma to a politician. Once given, they can only be enriched, never reduced or truncated. Once given to some, they then must be given to all. Votes are garnered by enriching the benefits to constituents. Those elected officials who understood the pending disaster and proposed amendments were crucified by their political opponents who capitalized on the opportunity to convince the electorate that their incumbent was attempting to eliminate benefits to which they were rightfully entitled. How can anyone have the audacity to reduce benefits to the poor, the elderly, the working man, the unemployed, or any other identifiable group?

Congress was fully aware of the potential disaster facing the social security program. Committee discussions were held throughout the sixties and early seventies to discover solutions. However, no politician entertained the thought of modifying eligibility or reducing benefits. All were more focused on discovering new things to tax, ways to develop the needed additional funding.

The short-term solution they legislated was an increase in the FICA payroll cap. Inflation was pushing salaries to levels that were significantly higher than anticipated when the prior FICA cap was set. Congress felt justified in passing an upward adjustment that mandated FICA contributions from both the employee and employer beyond the modest level that had applied earlier. Many employees previously reaching the FICA payroll cap in June or July were now contributing most of the year. The legislation also imbedded an upward scale for future increases in order to keep pace with anticipated wage inflation. The dollar increase the FICA collected was significant. Congress felt they had a win-win scenario. They successfully collected significantly greater tax revenue, and by removing this revenue from general circulation, they were also fighting inflation.

Funding entitlements to an ever-increasing number of recipients was causing the national debt to increase at a frightening rate. Revenue was lagging due to a struggling economy. Spending was soaring as funding for the massive volume of social welfare programs was commanding a greater and greater percentage of the annual expenditures. What could be done to mitigate the debt? Those who controlled our monetary fund found a solution … double-digit inflation. Borrow money today, then inflate the currency 12 percent per year, and in five years you effectively pay only half the debt. What the dollar bought in 1970 terms would cost two dollars in 1975. What a wonderful concept. Borrow to spend. Spend all you can because it will cost more next year, and you can pay back the loan with inflated dollars! The best part of this concept was quickly realized by our enlightened politicians; no one seemed to mind. Wages were increasing (for those that had work), home values were soaring (great for those who owned homes), and company sales volume had a built-in increase. Everyone who had a job was earning more every year and spending 120 percent of their raise, knowing they would pay back the debt with inflated dollars. What a solution for the government. Inflation meant more income-tax revenue, more sales-tax revenue, and more excise-tax revenue (collected as a percentage of items such as gasoline, liquor, cigarettes, etc.). Awesome fuel for a spending machine. Why not build in inflation as a normal condition? Government-inspired inflation was becoming imbedded into the national economic fabric. A new automobile that cost $5,000 in 1975 would cost $25,000 in 1985. Inflation became the solution that allowed our politicians holding office in the 1970s and 1980s to kick the can down the road.

During the Carter administration, double-digit inflation became the creative solution to finance the fiscally irresponsible legislation that was the cornerstone of the New Deal and the centerpiece of the Great Society.

CHAPTER 9

The Obama Takeovers

Let's now advance to 2008. What institutions remained in the American economy that were not totally controlled by the federal bureaucracy? What opportunities remained for the federal government to control or nationalize institutions in the name of fairness to the middle class? Who remained to be vilified for making too much money? Obama entered office with a mission in mind. Bankers, doctors, and every Wall Street trader became the declared enemy of the Obama nation. He mission was to contain their greed and curtail their ability to earn outrageous salaries. Entering office in the midst of a once-in-a-generation economic depression, Obama seized upon the opportunity (just as FDR had) to rally support to his cause.

His initial assault was on Wall Street and the big banks. The financial crises caused by the mortgage crisis required a federal bailout to save the economy. Obama and the Democrat-controlled Congress led by Nancy Pelosi leveraged the emotion associated with the bailout of the too-big-to-fail banks to pass legislation designed to control Wall Street. The response came in the form of the Dodd-Frank banking bill. This legislation imposed the most significant restraints on the American financial services business since FDR's New Deal. Dodd-Frank represents a significant change in the American financial regulatory environment, affecting all federal financial regulatory agencies and almost every aspect of the nation's financial-services industry. The bill also contained the first federal authority in the insurance industry. Dodd-Frank established the Federal Insurance Office within the Department of Treasury.

Obama, following the FDR model, successfully leveraged widespread panic into more federal control and more bureaucracy. Progressive liberals had long lamented the failure to seize total control of the banking during the first hundred days of the FDR administration. Now they not only successfully gained control of the banking industry but also gained a foothold in control of the insurance industry as well. The total impact of this legislation is yet to be seen. However, it is very clearly an attack on the financial-services industry. The federal bureaucracy will now oversee the financial-services industry with a mission to protect the consumer from all perceived abuses.

Obama and his Democratic cohorts then turned their sights on the medical delivery system. Democrats had long recognized the industry was not sufficiently contained for their taste. Since the FDR/New Deal days, Democrats acknowledged their desire to legislate a national health insurance program. Medicare and Medicaid legislation passed as an element of Johnson's Great Society contained a degree of cost control for the Medicare/Medicaid recipients. The Democrats soon realized controlling only a portion of the total medical expenditures was not sufficient to prevent cost shifting to other programs. Private health insurance, workers' compensation programs, and auto no-fault plans faced higher costs as the medical delivery system increased fully insured charges to offset the inadequacies in the Medicare/Medicaid reimbursements paid by the federal programs.

Obama, following FDR's political tradition of assaulting the assets of successful Americans (as mentioned earlier, FDR actually proposed an income tax rate of 100 percent for any earned income over $100,000) was determined to limit the financial opportunities available to the medical profession. Doctors and other related medical professionals have a long history of superior incomes. To the jealous politicians, the traditional level of income tax generated from the high-six-figure incomes doctors frequently earn is not sufficient to permit these seemingly unjustified income levels to continue. Most progressive politicians longed for a means to control the medical delivery system intending to contain cost and protect the common man. Our post–New Deal politicians apparently embrace the concept that free enterprise has no place in any operation that impacts the general public. Somehow the average American has come to believe that the control and oversight of our illuminated politicians (who believe they know more about every enterprise than the experienced entrepreneurs working in that business venture) can assure proper delivery of products and services to those who are entitled to receive them.

The average American has rejected the concept of universal health care delivered through a federally controlled medical delivery system. How then can the desires of the mainstream Democrats to institute this universal health care be met without the support of the plurality? The answer is Obamacare. Legislate mandatory coverage delivered through the existing health insurance system, and then use the legislation to regulate the entire process—insurance product design, treatment protocols, employer contributions, insurance carrier loss ratio levels, fines for noncompliance with the individual coverage mandate. And much, much more!

Comprehensive oversight and control gives the illusion of allowing the private sector to still run the medical delivery system. The federal mandates are so comprehensive, and embedded taxes and surcharges are so extensive, that they effectively eliminate all competitive factors that formerly differentiated private-sector medical delivery systems. The Obamacare legislation also created the opportunity to establish a federally operated alternative market to provide coverage to those individuals that could not obtain affordable coverage (state and federal exchanges). Aggressive amendments to the comprehensive health care bill will eventually drive more and more subscribers into this alternative market. Restricted medical reimbursement levels to doctors and hospitals paired with mandatory treatment protocols within the alternate market will eventually make this government-run program an effective price competitor to the private sector. Over time, these government-managed exchanges will become the primary insurance provider. Once in control of the majority of subscribers, this government alternative will set income levels for all medical service providers operating in the system. Salaries and benefits payable to physicians, nurses, anesthesiologists, and other support technicians will be rigidly set by the federal health insurer. Treatment protocols will be created for every ailment with controls in place to enforce compliance. No choice of doctors, no choice of treatment. Extensive cost containment will continue to narrow the choices and restrict treatment in a manner that would never be tolerated in the private market. Medical providers will avoid patients enrolled in the federal program to avoid the controls. However, within a reasonably short time frame, the significant premium differential between the federal program and private insurers will drive the majority of subscribers into the federal program. The individual mandate to obtain health insurance coverage will impose an obligation to provide valid proof of coverage on every individual in America. Given a choice to pay premium on a lower-cost federal program rather than continue with a private insurer, most will migrate to the lower cost despite the substantial restrictions. The migration of low-cost-seeking subscribers to the federal program will generate even greater the price differential. Soon the politicians will have what they wanted all along—everyone enrolled in a national health insurance program.

PART 3

Freefare

Mission accomplished! Every industry and every employer will be operating in an environment totally controlled by the federal bureaucracy. Total control on wages, bonuses, employee benefits, investments, borrowing, and pension plans. The New Deal and Great Society have successfully crossed the finish line. Karl Marx would be proud.

CHAPTER 10

Establishing Freefare

Before we introduce the concept of Freefare, let's review the way the political control evolved over the centuries.

Beginning in medieval times, those in a position of power employed fear as their primary control mechanism. National leaders rose to their status by controlling superior militaristic power, and the one with the fiercest army ruled. For centuries, *conquer, subjugate, and control with fear* was embraced by all as accepted theory of government control.

Acceptance of the theory of the divine right of kings gradually served to replace fear and military subjugation. Loyalty to the crown and strict adherence to religion worked for centuries. During this age, the theory of government and political leadership evolved to become *inherit power, opiate with religion, and control with loyalty to the crown and the church.*

Over time, the general population gradually came to be more and more educated. As the masses gained enlightenment, the ordained status of the royals came into question while at the same time blind acceptance of strict religious doctrine became less common. During the late seventeenth century, a major shift in the theory of government began to take root. The theory was crystalized at the beginning of the American Revolution: governments exist at the consent of the governed. The stated theory was based upon the notion that the general population of any nation held the ultimate authority to determine how they were to be governed, and they were also free to determine who was to do the governing. Fear, coercion, and blind obedience to church and state were no longer the acceptable means to sustain power.

The postrevolution American democracy became the shining best example of how to maintain consent. Establishment of regularly occurring elections allowed the new democracy to develop to meet the demands of the electorate. The majority vote determined the political direction of the nation. The American election process gave voice to the multitude. Individuals hoping to be elected joined political parties formed to focus support for or against social issues. The politician, with the support of his political party, solicited the support of the voters, selling their brand of solutions to the voters. Majority ruled, and political/social solutions were achieved at the consent of the governed rather than at the pleasure of the monarch.

During the late nineteenth century and the early twentieth century, this voting process established an updated expectation of government. Enlightened societies continued to emerge, and the developed world began to demonstrate that they were no longer willing to ignore the plight of the disenfranchised. The majority of the general population recognized that people fighting for survival presented a significant threat to the safety and well-being of society. Fearing the potential violence, the voting majority began to demand relief for those who were suffering.

The early twentieth century would clearly demonstrate the threat that desperate people represent. Starvation and the lack of hope gave rise to Hitler, Stalin, and FDR. All three achieved power by promising to relieve the suffering of the common man. The have-nots eagerly embraced champions who were committed to leading the battle against the haves. The worldwide chaos and the resulting World War accompanying the triumvirate's rise to power clearly demonstrated the consequences of ignoring those in need.

All post–World War II world leaders came to understand the threat the lower class presented. Societal classes with nothing left to lose organized into political groups, and trade unions became a formidable obstacle to maintaining power. The key to controlling these groups centered on the emerging theory that all governments owe an acceptable level of existence to everyone residing within their jurisdiction. To be successful in this mission, modern governments must guarantee that any overaccumulation of wealth be taxed (seized by the government) and properly redistributed to those at the lower rungs of the economic ladder. There was no mandate to determine why those occupying the lower end of the economic spectrum were in that position. Regardless of the cause or the reason, society dictated that the disenfranchised were entitled to a meaningful existence. By the end of World War II, the accepted theory of government had to be amended to recognize that consent of the governed required leadership to recognize the demands of the disenfranchised.

After World War II, a new modernized theory of government reached for a higher level of social responsibility by incorporating the concept that the primary mission of all national governments is to allocate wealth and resources among the governed; a meaningful and fair allocation (or reallocation) system must be implemented and enforced if long-term political stability is to be maintained.

FDR's New Deal proved best at delivering on the promise of serving the needs of the common man. While the American Revolution established the theory that all governments exist at the consent of the governed, FDR would author the modern amendment to that theory. His New Deal represented a clear demonstration that delivering benefits to the governed would henceforth become the ideal method to maintain political power. His administration demonstrated that an effective leader could essentially buy the consent of the governed.

In the post–New Deal era, the mission of all politicians became *get elected, opiate with benefits, and maintain control by delivering an increasing level of those benefits.*

Freefare is the ultimate manifestation of FDR and LBJ's dream of taking care of those that occupy the bottom rungs of the economic ladder. It will enhance the quality of life for every American occupying the have-not class of society and permanently remove them as a threat to society.

Freefare, once established, will also eliminate a significant portion of the established political bureaucracy. Freefare will significantly improve the efficiency of the operating system designed to deliver America's quality-of-life guarantee to everyone existing on our soil. No eligibility rules, no food stamps, no welfare checks. No more suffering, no more hunger, no more racial disparity. Slums will disappear, street gangs will be a thing of the past, and criminal activity will be virtually eliminated. Efficient redistribution of wealth while maintaining sufficient control over the recipients can be best achieved through the Freefare system.

America is now firmly entrenched in the age of entitlement. There is no turning back. The preceding chapters documented how we got here; we now must ask, where are we going?

The only viable path to the future leads directly to the concept of Freefare. Freefare will soon become normal state of the union. It represents the Holy Grail for all our socially responsible liberal politicians. Freefare is the penultimate form of governmental assistance with the added benefit of establishing a functioning system to exert a significant level of control over the entitlement recipients.

What is Freefare? What will our society look like once Freefare becomes the standard? What will be done to finance and sustain the program? How much Freefare will be tolerated? Who will want to work? Will the program ever end?

Read on and see!

CHAPTER 11

Freefare in Operation

Freefare will establish meaningful existence to every American, providing a path to social equality based on governmental benevolence. Full financial support will be given to anyone who decides they can't or don't want to work.

Future politicians elected by the entitled majority will be mandated to find sufficient funds to keep their promise of enhanced entitlements growing. These future entitlement politicians, confident in their majority position, will be anxious to impose their will on the American working class. They will force working Americans to accept new legislation and new taxes that require them to step up and accept their full measure of social responsibility. Their rhetoric will sound like this: "Why should anyone be allowed to live in an enormous house with three cars and a boat when there are children that go to bed hungry? The tax rate must be too low if so many Americans can live in such luxury!" These entitlement politicians collectively state, "It is time for the American working class to reach the understanding that they thrive only because the federal government allows them to perform and keep most of what they earn."

Business entrepreneurs will be forced to endure repeated assaults on their exorbitant profits. The entitled majority will make it clear to all business owners that the opportunity to establish and operate a business occurs only at the benevolence of the government. After all, government created (or allowed the creation of) most of the infrastructure—streets, roads, water systems, sewer systems, and communication lines—upon which the business depends. Without the benevolence of the government, the business would not survive. Government created the opportunity and continues to support and maintain the needed infrastructure. Therefore, it is only fair that the business owners accept their full measure of social responsibility.

The entitled majority will force everyone earning income to give in and take care of the underprivileged and unmotivated. Once the concession is made, the economics of the undertaking will require the process to be completed in the most efficient manner possible. Freefare is the answer—the full manifestation of the mature form of the entitlement mentality. Implementation of Freefare will totally eliminate the concept of being poor in America. Once in place, nothing new will be required to enrich the lives of the needy and underprivileged.

Initial efforts to subsidize the needy, labeled "welfare," were intended to be governmental assistance for those who were unable to work do to unfortunate circumstances. What welfare has always missed is the means to provide economic support to healthy Americans who cannot find work to match their current skill set or who just do not want to work.

Freefare eliminates the oversight. Just declare that you do not want to work, and you're in. No need to lie or cheat. Just declare that you want to be taken care of, and the federal government steps in to fill the need. Imagine the votes a future politician could attract with that concept. He could campaign on the slogan: No work and pay! How could anyone oppose that? Financing the program? Think about the millions of dollars that could be saved by eliminating the bureaucracy that currently functions to oversee the welfare system. Thousands of bureaucrats will be eliminated along with their bloated salaries, generous fringe benefits, and enormous pension plans. Freefare will prove that it is far more efficient to allocate funds currently expended on bureaucracy directly to the needy.

Here is how the initial enrollment in Freefare will work. A short visit to the Freefare office will set you up. Just declare that you don't feel like working, or you can't find a job you like, or you want more time with your family (literally any reason), and the process begins. Without any type of eligibility questions, applications for Freefare benefits will be simple and easily processed. The Freefare payouts are quickly initiated and begin without any hearings or investigations. No need to show cause or confirm disability or illness. Just complete the forms and become the ward of the state. The federal government will take care of you just like your mom and dad.

The first rule of Freefare is that it will be a totally cashless system. Governmental officials have long known the use of cash offers a high degree of untraceable purchase freedom. Using cash virtually eliminates the government's ability to monitor, control, and tax transactions. That's why drug dealers always use cash! Freefare eliminates the participant's spending freedom by requiring all recipients to repudiate the use of any form of cash. Cash will be restricted to those Americans not participating in Freefare. Once Freefare becomes the accepted American support system for those in need, all cash expenditures will require the user to provide proper identification to prove they are a non-Freefare consumer. Merchants, service providers, and banks will be required to maintain records of all cash transactions and report the use to a federal cash control board. The newly established Federal Cash Use Control Board will be charged with the duty to monitor and control all use of cash and verify that the cash user is an authorized user. No Freefare participant will ever be allowed to hold any cash!

Upon enrollment, the Freefare participants will be required to relinquish all access to cash. They will be required to close all bank accounts and surrender all existing funds in checking, savings, or investment accounts to the Freefare system. In exchange for this surrendering, all existing debt will be extinguished. The Freefare system will pay off all credit cards, car payments, and mortgages, even college loans, everything. Once all the recipient's accounts have been surrendered, any attempt by the recipient to participate in any form of cash transaction will cause the recipient to suffer a significant restriction of their nonessential Freefare benefits. The Freefare enrollee enters the system without cash but will be totally debt-free.

How then, without the use of cash, will the Freefare system deliver goods and services to the participant? The answer is very simple; all purchases will be made using a specifically designated debit card. Freefare debit cards will be issued to the enrollee, enabling the participant to pay all normal expenses associated with a meaningful quality of life using their debit cards.

Suddenly with a stroke of the legislative pen, an entirely new segment of the population will be provided the means to become voracious consumers. Their increased spending power will fuel the economy, generating more jobs and more tax revenue. The financial demands of the new Freefare system will be partially financed by the significant growth in tax revenue generated from soaring economic growth. An entire segment of the population, previously considered an economic drag on the economy, will become a meaningful economic force. Millions of Americans armed with a wallet full of government-funded debit cards will hit the streets ready to fill the stores.

Several classes of debit cards will be used. Multiple cards will be necessary as each general card category will be monitored and managed by a separate Freefare control system. The following is a sample of the potential debit card categories:

Housing. The housing debit card will be designed to cover all normal expenses associated with the residence of the enrollee. Freefare enrollees will not be allowed to own or reside in a private dwelling. If the enrollee owned and resided in a home at the time of application, the home is surrendered to the Freefare system. Any mortgage on a participant's existing home will be paid off using Freefare funds. That property will then be sold by the Freefare system, and the proceeds will be retained by the system. All Freefare recipients will be required to reside in an apartment. However, that apartment can be located in any part of any city. The limit on the size of the apartment will be determined by the size of the family occupying the unit. The apartment owner will be obligated to accept the Freefare enrollee and will not be allowed to disclose the Freefare status of the renter. Rent and all associated utilities will be paid using the Freefare housing debit card. The apartment owner and the utility companies no longer have to worry about collection. They will be guaranteed their payment every month via the debit card. There will no longer be a need for eviction notices or utility shutoff. Thousands of hours of court time will be alleviated. A Freefare Housing Board will monitor all expenditures and investigate any abnormal or unusual expenditure. If the review board believes the utility expenses are higher than normal, the board will investigate and require the landlord to make the adjustments recommended by the board. If the changes are not adopted, the board will reduce the rent to a lower amount equal to the appropriate offset for the abnormal utility expense. If the higher expense is a direct result of tenant activities, the control board will take the appropriate steps to bring the utility expense back in line.

Chapter 12 will discuss the advantages presented by the housing approach, including no more slum areas in big cities, no identification of the nonworking class, a quality environment in which to raise children, and so forth.

Vehicles. Each Freefare enrollee will be entitled to purchase a nonluxury private passenger vehicle of his or her choice. The vehicle can be purchased from any dealer in any city. The vehicle debit card will pay for the vehicle, any repairs, and all the fuel needed to operate the vehicle. The card will also cover the expense to purchase an adequate level of insurance coverage. Each enrollee will be entitled to a new vehicle every six years. The Freefare vehicle owner will be required to perform all regular maintenance and service work on the vehicle (all paid by the automobile debit card). The Freefare Vehicle Control Board will monitor all vehicle-related transactions (including adherence to normal service requirements) and address any deviations that may occur in fuel or maintenance expenditures. The advantages of the vehicle program will also be discussed in chapter 12.

Food and clothing. Within this category, the enrollee will be entitled to all of the food and clothing he or she normally needs (as determined by the Food and Clothing Control

Board). Purchases will be monitored by the Freefare Food and Clothing Control Board, an oversight unit that reviews the volume and type of purchases. Food types, volumes, and nutrition value of all food purchased will be monitored via the debit card. Each enrollee will be required to receive regular nutrition counseling as part of the Freefare wellness program. Specific intervention programs will be directed to those families that deviate from acceptable nutrition levels, identified by the purchases made on the debit card and the medical results identified in the recipient's wellness program. Rather than passing laws restricting the purchase of giant servings of soda, the well-meaning politician can simply forbid the purchase on the debit card. The clothing allowance will provide sufficient opportunity to dress the family in a manner such that the Freefare participant's economic status cannot be identified. Clothing types, stores used, and volume purchased will be monitored. Overuse or the purchase of clothing deemed inappropriate will motivate an intervention from the control board. Freefare counselors will interact with the participants on a regular basis to advise what is deemed to be the appropriate style and volume of clothing. Again, see chapter 12 for further discussion.

Entertainment. A preloaded debit card will be issued to provide the enrollee with a reasonable amount of entertainment. The card can be used for items such as movie tickets, televisions, games, iPods, computers, music, and sporting events. The limit on the card will not allow the recipient sufficient funds to purchase any season tickets to any sport or theatrical event, but it will have sufficient funds to attend a limited number of these events. The card will have a monitoring aspect overseen by the Freefare Entertainment Control Board that will allow for review of the use of the card to confirm that the recipient is using the funds in an appropriate manner. Inappropriate use (such as any attempt to use fund for gambling) will be subject to mandatory counseling. Repeated misuse will result in revocation of the card. The funds associated with this card will be considered privileged funds and will be adjusted periodically to reward full compliance with Freefare control boards.

Medical services. All Freefare participants will be enrolled in a Freefare medical insurance program. A selected private insurance carrier will provide coverage using a specific plan design developed by the Freefare Medical Control Board. Insurance policies will be issued, and all premiums will be paid by the participant using the medical debit card. The medical debit card will also pay any and all uncovered medical care costs, such as insurance deductibles, co-pays, and dental and eyewear expenses. Everyone will be fully covered with no out-of-pocket exposure.

Medical insurance premiums should begin to fall in both the Freefare and the private market as everyone in America will be insured. The need for premium surcharges or provider cost adjustments currently applied to subsidize the uninsured will be eliminated. Non-Freefare participants will continue to be required to purchase health insurance as first established in the Affordable Care Act (Obamacare). Premium taxes assessed to provide subsidies for welfare and Medicaid participants that are now hidden in the commercial health insurance premiums will no longer be necessary. Everyone in America will be insured, either through private insurers providing employer-based or individual policies in the standard insurance market or in the Freefare program. The subsidized Obamacare policies that use Medicare reimbursement rates to pay medical service providers will be eliminated, allowing all providers to return to profitability. Insurance affordability for the poor will no longer be an issue, and the billions of dollars spent on premium subsidies will be redirected to the Freefare program.

The Freefare Medical Control Board will oversee the entire medical services segment, including provider selection, insurance plan design, primary care physician selection, and final approval for any major medical procedures. To keep costs down, every Freefare participant will be required to enroll in a medical wellness program regularly monitored by the Freefare Medical Control Board. Wellness programs will include gym memberships, nutrition classes, smoking cessation counseling, and online interactive weight management programs. Failure to comply with the mandatory wellness initiatives will be reported to the Freefare medical oversight unit, and specific counseling will be directed to the noncompliant family or individual. The combination of a fully insured population and mandated compliance with wellness initiatives will produce a healthier population, thus reducing the overall cost of the Freefare health insurance premiums.

Freefare health insurance subscribers will have full prescription coverage. However, prescriptions will be restricted to generic brands. If any doctor believes a brand-name drug is required, the doctor must refer the case for clearance. The Freefare Medical Control Board will also negotiate with all the generic drug manufacturers to obtain significant price reductions. The board will develop a specific prescription protocol for each ailment and mandate a specific generic drug for treatment of the defined ailment. Significant discounts will be gained when the control board negotiates with the generic manufacturer to become the exclusive provider for the selected prescription treatment. For example, there are hundreds of different drugs available to treat urinary tract infections in women. The board would study outcomes, select the most effective drug to treat the ailment, and then designate the selected drug manufacturer the exclusive provider for prescription treatment of urinary tract infections. The board would then negotiate a significant discount from the drug manufacturer. Periodic reviews will confirm the effectiveness of the drug. All medical providers (doctors, emergency rooms, clinics) must prescribe the selected drug, or it will be rejected and substituted at the drugstore.

The Freefare health insurance program will require the doctor to electronically submit every serious case to the Freefare Medical Control Board to receive treatment approval and to obtain a mandatory treatment protocol to manage the observed condition. The doctor will be required to treat the condition according to the protocol response he receives. Should he elect to follow some alternative treatment protocol, the doctor will not be paid. The Freefare Medical Control Board will be in total control of all treatments for all subscribers enrolled in the Freefare insurance plan. The control board will be charged with reviewing every potential serious medical condition, analyzing all treatment options, then having exclusive authority to mandate the treatment procedure that will produce the best overall outcome (medically and financially). Once the board selects the best treatment to control a specific condition, they will have total authority to enforce the selected procedure. No variations will be tolerated. Doctors refusing to use the authorized treatment protocol will not be paid and will have no recourse to collect from the Freefare participant. Should a physician uncover a condition that does not have an established treatment protocol, the physician must submit the file to the control board and wait for board instruction regarding treatment before commencing.

The Freefare health insurer, treating doctors, and all conforming medical service providers will be exempt from any medical malpractice claims arising from treatment prescribed to Freefare subscribers. All Freefare subscribers will also sign a treatment waiver that authorizes the Freefare Medical Control Board to become the exclusive proxy to determine appropriate treatment of any and all conditions. The medical malpractice exemption and the treatment waiver will eliminate the need for unnecessary defensive procedures and testing.

The death panels discussed during the Obamacare debates will indeed be created and become an additional function of the Freefare Medical Control Board. The treatment waiver signed by the subscribers will allow the control board exclusive authority to withhold or terminate treatment for conditions that are determined to be ineffective in curing the patient or restoring that patient to a useful life. The control board will also be authorized to euthanize those subscribers who are determined to be unable to return to a useful life condition.

Wellness programs will be mandatory for Freefare health insurance subscribers. Every subscriber will be assigned a health coach who will be charged with determining all appropriate lifestyle adjustments that they may deem necessary to address subscriber health risks. Nutrition, weight management, exercise programs, smoking cessation, preventative medications, and many other tools will be used to manage subscriber health conditions. The Freefare participants who fail to comply with the wellness programs outlined by their health coach will forfeit debit card entertainment dollars.

Overall, oversight by the Freefare Medical Control Board should significantly reduce the cost of medical services provided to Freefare participants. Coverage provided is totally free, so the compliance requirements cannot be objected to. Cost containment will become a major consideration. The control board will have full authority to implement all treatment protocols they deem appropriate to achieve their cost objectives.

Private-market health insurance will remain in existence after the Freefare health insurance program commences. The private market insurers will continue to offer group programs to employers as well as individual coverage for those unemployed subscribers not participating in Freefare. These private-market insurers will function as traditional providers. They will not be exempt from medical malpractice suits, and there will be no mandatory wellness programs, no death panels, and no mandatory treatment protocols. The premiums will be higher than the Freefare premium financed by the government, but the Freefare Medical Control Board will have no input. In the private market, the doctor and the patient will retain control over all treatment protocols. Wellness will continue to be voluntary, and the death panels will not exist. Employers will be permitted to continue to make tax-deductible contributions to premium. However, any employer contribution to premium will become taxable income to the employee/subscriber.

Retaining control over medical treatment protocols and coverage options will become one of the primary motivators for individuals to continue working (or to find work) and refrain from enrolling in the Freefare program.

Chapter 12 will outline the benefit of wellness programs, preventative care, and early intervention to the overall cost of this portion of the program.

Education. The Freefare education debit card will cover any expenses associated with any form of education attempted by the enrollee and his family. Expenses include school supplies and any related expenses associated with public school education. Private schools at a level of grade twelve or below will not be allowed. All education outcomes will be reviewed by a Freefare Education Control Board. The board will have the power to step in and intercede if there are any issues with a Freefare student. The card will cover any and all expenses (including housing) incurred by the participant while attending any college or university. The costs associated with their attendance will be funded by a special assessment to the attended college endowment fund. There will no longer be any barriers for any disenfranchised individual to receive the highest form of education available. The free education aspect will remove any and all barriers to self-improvement opportunity. Should Freefare recipients wish to pursue higher education in an attempt to exit the system, the opportunity will be available to attend any institution of higher education they may choose, totally free of charge. The education program will include mandatory work-orientation programs. The primary objective will be to encourage the Freefare student to enter the workforce after graduation. Should students enter the workforce, they will do so without any debt obligation for their education. The hope would be that the free education plan would serve to effectively reduce Freefare participation over time.

There you have it. Every entitlement anyone would need to live a quality life equally available to all with just a swipe of a debit card. It will no longer be necessary to live in a rundown slum and dress in tattered clothing. No excuse (in fact no opportunity) to eat a nutritionally poor meal. Comprehensive medical services and advanced education in the country's best institutions provided for free to everyone in the system. Freefare participants will be impossible to identify by sight; they will simply blend in with everyone in the neighborhood. It will be impossible to identify participants by their manner of dress or the neighborhood in which they live. No more slums, no need to raise a family in the hood. Every recipient will have the opportunity to dress well, eat well, get educated, and be cared for medically.

The two biggest questions about the Freefare program will be, how will all of this be funded and who will want to work?

The price tag for Freefare will be enormous. What type of tax will be levied to provide the funding? Who will continue working only to pay more tax? The answer is simple. There will be no new taxes needed. Freefare will be financed in a number of ways:

1) Through the tremendous increase in tax revenue generated through an exploding economy that will be fueled by the new Freefare consumption
2) By redirecting funds from existing overlapping, redundant programs like food stamps, welfare, subsidized housing, and a number of other social services programs
3) By eliminating the bloated politically appointed bureaucracy that previously provided administrative services to outdated programs
4) By redirecting the numerous subsidies and hidden tax in the current health insurance programs
5) By eliminating Medicare
6) By eliminating Medicaid
7) By removing all Freefare participants from social security
8) By eliminating unused retirement funds from individual estates (Remaining balances

in accumulated retirement funds that were accumulated tax-free, such as pension plans, 401K plans, IRA plans, will be taxed 100 percent.)

9) Through sizable reductions in budgets directed toward crime and crime prevention, urban development, drug enforcement, and crime rehabilitation programs

10) By reworking the income-tax code into a wealth-distribution system that places earning caps on businesses and individuals (Income earned above the cap level will be usurped by the federal government and redistributed to the Freefare program.)

Let's start by considering the significantly higher tax revenues generated from the economic growth arising from the increase in consumer spending by the Freefare recipients. Apartment owners will prosper, auto sales will skyrocket, and groceries, clothing, electronics, and other consumable products will see unbelievable sales growth as the Freefare recipient engages the multiple debit cards. The job growth (for those that choose to work) to support the new demand will be record setting, generating enormous increases in income taxes collected. Economists will no longer track the unemployment rate, replacing it with statistics on the number of unfilled available jobs. Wages will rise as Freefare will limit the available supply of employees, and employers will have to pay more and provide richer benefits to attract and retain employees. The need for a minimum-wage law will be eliminated as the employed worker will opt for Freefare if the going wage is not sufficient to provide all the essentials. Corporate profits will soar, payrolls will soar, and with it, the taxes generated will be at levels never seen before.

The current social services landscape is filled with thousands of overlapping, redundant assistance programs designed to benefit narrow segments of the underprivileged population. Freefare will eliminate all of these programs along with their support bureaucracy.

Health insurance premiums are loaded with numerous taxes and surcharges designed to subsidize the uninsured and to help fund Medicaid and other subsidy programs. Freefare will eliminate the need for such programs, and the taxes and surcharges can be directed directly to Freefare.

The Medicare program will disappear, as all former participants will receive their medical benefits through the Freefare system. Medicare reform accomplished by enhancing it. Just the ticket for the future politician. Every Freefare participant will already be fully covered by a Freefare medical insurance program with all premiums paid through a Freefare debit card. Freefare medical continues from initial enrollment until death. New legislation will require the private insurance providers that service the Freefare program to cover all illnesses, accidents, and diseases. Everything is covered, No preexisting conditions will be excluded. If a working family and not currently enrolled in the Freefare program faces uninsured catastrophic medical bills, they can simply give up and enroll in the Freefare program. Everything will be taken care of, and all medical debt will be forgiven. No more Medicare. No more Medicaid. No more providers complaining about the low levels of Medicare reimbursements. No more Medicare shortfall cost shifting to the private insurers. Everything will be provided through private insurers administering a federally backed program. The Medicare and Medicaid bureaucracy will be eliminated. All administration involving enrollment and oversight will be handled through the Freefare Medical Control Board.

Here is how Freefare will eventually eliminate the Medicare program. The Freefare system will contain no eligibility age restrictions for the insurance coverage. Those Freefare participants who reach age sixty-five merely continue their existing Freefare medical insurance. Premiums for the Freefare subscribers regardless of age will be paid via the Freefare debit card. Appropriate premium development systems will continue to reflect actuarially sound rating factors, including age. The large number of older individuals participating in the insurance plan will allow the insurer to properly set an actuarially correct rate. The insurance providers covering the Freefare recipients will benefit from the increased premium flows generated from the premium retained by the company for the over-sixty-five-year-old subscribers that formerly dropped out and enrolled in Medicare. Calculation of appropriate rating factors will eliminate the need for any rate subsidy assessed to healthier rating segments. The resulting age-weighted rates and premiums will not be an issue for the Freefare participants, as the government pays 100 percent of the premium.

Those individuals who chose work over Freefare will retain coverage they were provided through their employer's group program for the remainder of their life. Legislation will be passed requiring the insurer covering the employee when the employee chose to retire to continue coverage until death. The premium is paid by the individual (it's possible that future employers may subsidize part of the retirement health insurance cost as part of their employee benefit plan). The only means of cancellation will be for nonpayment of premium. Retired former workers will be required to provide continuous proof of insurance similar to the auto insurance requirement that currently exists in most states. Premiums for the non-Freefare participants will be the responsibility of the subscriber, using tax-deductible premium payments presumably paid from their retirement funds that in the Freefare future will become a use-it-or-lose-it benefit anyway.

The recent trend toward health savings accounts (HSAs) will accelerate as those individuals who choose to work will be motivated to accumulate funds in the HSA accounts to assist them during retirement. To encourage the accumulation of funds in the health savings accounts, legislation will be passed to increase the maximum limit for tax-deductible contributions to a level well above the current limitation. The new legislation will also allow the individual to pay postretirement premiums from the HSA account. Those that cannot afford the postretirement premiums can always elect the option to abdicate all assets and enroll in the Freefare system if retirement funds run out. The elimination of Medicare will eliminate the cost shifting associated with the current environment. The requirement that everyone be fully insured will also eliminate the subsidies required to fund the uninsured. The trillions of dollars currently allocated to the Medicare program within the federal budget will be eliminated and allocated instead to the Freefare system.

Think of the billions of dollars that are associated with Medicare. Then double the obligation as the baby boomer generation reaches age sixty-five. It doesn't take a rocket scientist to understand that a program that provides comprehensive medical coverage, including prescription benefits, for a monthly premium of less than a hundred dollars is not economically feasible. The debt crisis that currently exists will only get worse without substantial modifications to the Medicare program. Freefare will allow the kick-the-can-down-the-road politicians a way out. Overall, health insurance premiums should fall as the number of those insured skyrockets and all subsidies associated with insufficient Medicare and Medicaid reimbursements and the added cost funding for the uninsured disappear.

Increased implementation of insurance programs like the high-deductible health plans that incorporate a health savings accounts will add a tax-free method of financing future insurance costs for those that choose to work. The Medicare surcharge for both the employer and the employee can be eliminated with the resulting savings applied to insurance premiums. It may even be feasible that employers, given the appropriate tax incentives, would be willing to participate in the cost of the postretirement premiums required from their former employees. It would be a reasonable assumption to assume that the health insurance premiums paid by younger, healthier, working individuals would fall dramatically as all the uninsured and Medicare-related subsidies would be eliminated.

Transition to the new program should be relatively quick and easy. Existing Medicare recipients can be grandfathered in and allowed to eventually run off. Workers approaching retirement age will be legislatively required to continue coverage with their existing insurer, most likely the insurance carrier that provides the group coverage for their employer. The cost of the insurance will be made tax deductible for the retiree. Employers can also choose to contribute tax-deductible dollars to subsidize retiree premiums. Those older retirees who were not provided sufficient time to save for retirement premiums will be given subsidies to help pay premiums. Freefare and modified retirement legislation will allow Medicare to phase out.

Next we can look at social security. Everyone knows this program has been in financial crises since the early sixties.

The program cannot be sustained at its current contribution levels. Something must be done. However, every politician that has proposed changes that reduce or limit payments has been crucified by the opposing party. The only politically sound method to alter the program is to enhance it. Or at least to appear to enhance it. Freefare is the answer. Freefare will have no age restrictions. Anyone reaching age sixty-five can enter the system by forgoing all assets and future claims to social security income. Those who are already in the Freefare program merely continue until they pass away.

With Freefare in place, the social security program can be modified to apply only to those who actually work and contribute to the program. The plan can easily be converted to an alternative funding system in which some or all of the funds contributed to the social security program could become self-directed and merged with existing 401K or pension plans (remember all funds that remain upon death will be forfeited to the federal government). Younger participants could totally opt out of the social security plan by fully participating in employer-based retirement plans that meet minimum standards set by the Social Security Administration. Middle-aged participants can continue with the existing program or accept a buyout where a lump sum is transferred from social security into an existing pension plan or IRA. The buyout will be discounted to reflect potential future pension plan earnings. The buyout will also incorporate catch-up provisions that will allow the employee the opportunity to direct additional tax-deferred funds into the pension/IRA programs. Within a few decades, social security as it currently exists will disappear and will be fully replaced with mandatory retirement contributions made by both the employee and the employer. Consider the benefits. Eliminating the FICA contribution will free up funds for both the employee and the employer.

Federal legislation will require most of the savings to go to retirement plans. The growth in the pension/IRA marketplace will skyrocket. The avalanche of new funds into the plans will create sizable growth in funds available for investment. These funds can be used to fuel economic growth. Retirement funds withdrawn for retirement funding from the booming retirement plans will remain taxable income to the recipient. Retirees will gain additional tax deductions for funding medical and dental insurance to help offset the significant increase in annual taxable distributions generated from the new use-it-or-lose-it status of the funds. Consider the dramatic growth in tax revenue generated from future retirees. Freefare modifications to the inheritance tax that eliminate the ability to transfer retirement funds to any beneficiary other than the current spouse will force individuals to take higher annual distributions and will also allow the federal government to capture all the remaining retirement fund balances once the recipient passes away. Everyone wins. Everyone is happy, and social security as it currently exists disappears. Think of the billions of dollars saved by dissolving the social security bureaucracy.

Now consider the trillions of dollars that have accumulated pretax in tax-free retirement accounts. Revenue-hungry politicians will tell you they allowed these funds to accumulate to finance retirement. Our politicians will tell everyone that it was never their intent to allow individuals to develop substantially large estates within these retirement plans. The purpose of the funds was to provide retirement income to the plan participant. The current estate tax codes allow the accumulation of these tax-free funds to be passed on to selected heirs as part of an individual's estate. It will only take a swipe of the presidential pen to make all of these retirement funds a noninheritable asset.

In the future Freefare world, retirement funds for non-Freefare participants can be withdrawn after retirement at will (on a taxable basis) during the retirement years (after age 59 and a half) of the individual and their spouse. (All Freefare participants relinquish 100 percent of any retirement funds once they enroll in the Freefare plan.) When the retirement fund holder and his or her spouse pass away, all funds remaining in their retirement account will be forfeited to the federal government—a 100 percent remaining-balance tax. Retirement funds (pension, IRA, and 401K plans) will become a totally noninheritable asset. Spend it and pay taxes or lose the balance upon death. The potential for this type of legislation may be closer than you think. The beauty of Freefare is that those retirees who run out of funds will avoid any financial consequences, as they will be allowed to enroll in the Freefare program as soon as the funds run out. No risk—spend and enjoy retirement. The only risk will be the forfeit of equity in the home and any other marketable assets.

Now consider the billions of tax dollars that are spent on containing crime, drug enforcement, financing urban development, subsidizing medical care for the uninsured, payroll for the welfare bureaucracy, food stamps, school lunch programs, rental assistance programs, tuition assistance, and a laundry list of other public assistance programs both federal and state. Freefare will eliminate the need for all of these programs.

The liberal politicians, the new progressives, will tell the public that the government funding for the Freefare programs will be more efficiently redirected directly to those who elect to be wards of the state.

The economic growth resulting from the debit card purchases made by the Freefare recipients will generate a significant increase in federal tax revenues. Purchases of vehicles, clothing, furniture, and food will skyrocket. Construction of new apartment buildings and the demolition of old, rundown slums will create thousands of construction jobs. The resulting increase in demand will also fuel inflation. The skyrocketing inflation will make the current national debt a nonissue.

Developing other ultraliberal societal improvements could also serve to reduce crime. The first will likely be the legalization of drugs. The elimination of cash in the Freefare system will make it virtually impossible for the participant to purchase drugs. Every transaction using the Freefare debit card will be monitored, so any anomalies in spending habits that could indicate an unauthorized transaction, such as trading newly purchased items for drugs, will be immediately investigated by the control board. Once drug use is legalized distribution channels will collapse when our ultra-liberal society provides a method for everyone (including non-Freefare individuals) wishing to use recreational drugs to obtain his or her drug of choice for free by checking into a federally run free drug campus. The drug cartels will have a very difficult time competing with *free.*

Federally run drug-use campuses will be located in isolated rural areas, fenced in and patrolled to contain the inhabitants. Initially users will be provided intensive counseling, and total rehab will be encouraged. Every attempt will be made to dissuade the free drug user from his or her addiction. Once the inhabitant has failed to rehab and has fully committed to permanently using their drug of choice, they will be provided unlimited quantities at the facility. The free drug user will then be considered a permanent resident of the campus. Visitors will be allowed, but the resident will be restricted to the campus.

Another potential adjustment made to control crime will be the treatment of individuals choosing to commit a crime. The first offense perpetrated by a Freefare recipient could lead to a severe restriction of benefits (such as loss of vehicle and entertainment privileges). Benefits will be restored only after a sufficient number of mandatory crime counseling sessions have been completed. Any individual using a weapon in the commitment of a crime will immediately be conscripted into the military and sent to the front lines of any conflict existing at the time. There they will be appropriately allowed to satisfy their need to handle a weapon.

A second offense will remove the individual from his or her residence and require internment in a rehab facility for a period of time commensurate with the crime committed. While in the crime rehab facility, the perpetrator will be evaluated to determine specific treatment needs. A substantial effort will be put forth to rehabilitate the perpetrator.

After release from rehab, those committing a third offense will be permanently removed to a criminal campus where they will be retained for the remainder of their life. Criminal campuses like the free drug campus will be located in rural areas, fenced, and fully patrolled. They will be a milder version of the current prison system. This may seem harsh. However, keep in mind that all the economic incentives for crime will have been eliminated by the Freefare system, and specific counseling was provided during the interment to a treatment facility.

Freefare will eliminate the potential for any type of social upheaval. Slums will be torn down. Gangs will no longer be necessary. Cultural and racial economic differences will be eliminated.

The potential to obtain absolute control over the formerly disenfranchised individual is very appealing to governmental leaders. Through the monitoring of the expenditures arising from the Freefare debit cards and the outlawing of cash, federal officials know virtually every activity the recipient chooses to undertake. Karl Marx felt that religion was the opiate of the masses. To some extent it is. However, Freefare is the ultimate opiate. Keep everyone in a good environment, feed them and entertain them, and the masses will be subdued.

Consider the opportunity for future politicians to refine the Freefare system. Freefare control boards will have insight into every aspect of activity by Freefare recipients using systems that monitor the activities on the debit cards. Access to what type of food is purchased, what type of entertainment was watched, what type of clothing was purchased, and what type of vehicle is selected is only a computer click away. The opportunity to inject counseling for inappropriate activities (such as poor nutrition) into this system is a logical extension of the Freefare program. Elimination of cash will allow the various control boards to manage all purchases to the extent necessary to produce the desired outcome. Freefare is the vehicle our liberal society will use to create the ultimate nanny state.

The next logical question to ask—given all the benefits available under Freefare—is, who would actually want to work? What will become the motivation to hold a job?

The answer is related to the government control and oversight of every activity related to Freefare. Under Freefare, government agencies will monitor every activity undertaken by the Freefare recipient. Intervention will take place whenever any activity strays from the prescribed norm established by a federally appointed oversight board. Take for example the perceived obesity issue. Statistics indicate the average American is becoming more and more overweight. Several of our enlightened politicians have proposed imposing a substantial tax on junk food to curtail purchases, believing the tax would discourage consumption. Under Freefare, the process would be far more effective. The Food and Clothing Board that oversees the use of their debit card would be fully authorized to view all food purchases made using their debit card. If the board determines that the recipient is overspending on inappropriate food groups, they can intervene. Just click a few key strokes and the inappropriate food purchases will be blocked on the debit card. The Freefare recipient would also be enrolled into a mandatory nutrition counseling program. If any individual wants to avoid this level of control, they could always get a job.

Individuals holding a job would continue to maintain complete spending discretion. Employed persons would be free to use cash for their purchases (after showing the appropriate photo ID card). Using their earned income, they would be free to spend without limitations. Employed individuals would also be allowed to purchase homes and furnish them at their discretion. Employed individuals using cash and credit cards (for things like giant sodas) would avoid all governmental intervention from the Freefare Debit Card Oversight Board. The ability to spend without oversight or limitation will be a key motivation to maintain a job and a career.

The Freefare system will eliminate all inheritable assets from Freefare recipients. Only those who work will be able to maintain the financial freedom to create an estate. Freefare recipients will be required to forfeit all assets upon enrollment. This will include all checking and savings accounts, all homes and non-Freefare vehicles. All future purchases will be made using government-issued debit cards. No cash allowed. Nothing of value owned (all possessions such as clothing and vehicles surrendered to the Freefare system upon the passing of the participant). Nothing owned to pass on to children and grandchildren. Freefare recipients will have no assets to pass on!

Anyone wishing to build an estate and leave a legacy for children and grandchildren must work so that they can actually own property and accumulate funds in savings and investment accounts. Retirement funds such as pension, 401K, and IRA accounts will not be inheritable and will be held on a use-it-or-lose-it basis.

Chapter 12 will discuss the restructured view of society after Freefare is fully institutionalized. The benefits to society will be more fully outlined. However, consider just the crime issue. Freefare will supply all the primary necessities of life, so it will virtually eliminate the need to commit burglary and robbery to obtain them. Providing funding for apartment living in any selected neighborhood will eliminate low-income housing areas and urban slums. Poor neighborhoods controlled by gangs will be a thing of the past. Freefare recipients will not be allowed to hold or spend cash. All cash transactions will require a photo identification card confirming the person spending the cash is not participating in the Freefare program. Eliminating cash from the system will end the ability to convert government assistance into alcohol, drugs, or weapons.

Freefare is the perfect vehicle to control the masses. The have-nots will no longer exist. Spending oversight and administrative intervention will commence as soon as the debit card is used inappropriately. Big brother will be watching and prepared to step in whenever "help" is needed. Total social integration for all classes, all races, all genders, all ages. No slums, no high-crime areas, no poor people. The official Little League will be our societal image; everyone gets to play regardless of talent or motivation.

Read on to see how it works!

CHAPTER 12

A New Society with Freefare

To fully understand the transition to Freefare, we should consider the plight of Joe. Joe was born in Buffalo, New York. Joe's father, Carl, worked in the steel plant in Lackawanna, and his mother, Sally, dropped out of school when she became pregnant with Joe early in her senior year of high school. Carl and Sally were married shortly after they received confirmation of the pregnancy. They rented an apartment on Buffalo's South Side, and all went well until Joe turned eight. Carl lost his job when the steel plant closed. He was devastated and began to drink heavily. Within a year, Carl and Sally separated, and Sally had to apply for welfare in order to provide food and shelter for Joe. Sally was then forced by her circumstances to move to subsidized housing in a poor Buffalo neighborhood. Joe entered a world that was unfamiliar. Fearing for his safety, Joe joined a gang to survive. His whole life took a turn for the worse. His mother had turned to drugs and alcohol, and his gang was turning him into a criminal. He was at a crossroads. He was a high school dropout with no marketable employment skills. How would he survive?

Freefare was legislated into existence just in time. Joe enrolled immediately, and shockingly he obtained all the debit cards he needed to live a "normal" life. Immediately he rented an apartment in Hamburg, New York, an affluent suburb of Buffalo. He used the clothing debit card to buy a new wardrobe and the auto allowance to purchase a new car. There he was, well dressed, living in an affluent neighborhood, driving a new car. He became totally undistinguishable from anyone else in the neighborhood. Groceries in the cupboard, video game connected to the big screen, life was good. No need for a gang in this environment!

Shortly after he moved into his new apartment, Joe received a call from the Freefare Food and Clothing Control Board. It seems the board reviewed his initial food purchases on the debit card and considered them to be inappropriate. The board required Joe to set up a meeting with a board-appointed nutrition counselor. The counselor met with Joe, and the counselor set up a nutritionally sound meal program for Joe to follow. The counselor then took Joe to a local food market to demonstrate the types of groceries required to follow the newly established nutrition program. Appropriate groceries were purchased and brought back to Joe's new apartment. The counselor then removed all inappropriate food items found in Joe's kitchen and threw them in the trash. The counselor went on to give Joe instructions on food preparation and a computer flash drive that offered a number of popular recipes and meal preparation tips. Joe was then informed that his food and clothing debit card was no longer authorized for use in the purchase of inappropriate junk food. The flash drive given to Joe outlined most of the food types considered to be inappropriate and also listed a number of fast-food restaurants that were now unavailable on the debit card. Joe had no choice; follow the program or go hungry!

Next came the call from the Freefare Education Control Board. They were aware that Joe had dropped out of high school and did not hold a high school diploma. They made him aware of a special program for Freefare participants to go to classes and complete the high school curriculum. They told Joe that he was not obligated to attend but offered additional entertainment dollars as an incentive. They let Joe know that if he fulfilled the requirements for graduation, the board would provide a week-long, all-expenses-paid vacation as a reward. They also let Joe know that if he wished to enroll in any college of his choice after high school graduation, he could attend, and all expenses would be paid by the Freefare system.

Now compare Joe's situation with Sam, another Buffalo area youth that grew up in a far more affluent household. Sam grew up in Orchard Park, New York, a wealthy neighborhood just south of Buffalo. Sam's father, Robert, was an attorney, and his mother, Elizabeth, was an accountant. Sam was enrolled in a private school where he spent most of his time faking his way through most classes. Both parents worked long hours, so Sam had plenty of alone time after school. Sam used the time to smoke pot and play video games. Upon finishing the private high school, Sam's father made a significant donation to a local college to assure Sam's admission. Sam enrolled, but due to poor grades caused by lack of attendance, he lasted only one semester. He was also under suspicion of selling pot. However, his unacceptable grade point average got him kicked out before any disciplinary action was taken for the drug offense. Robert and Elizabeth were horrified and embarrassed. They disowned him and threw him out of the house, forcing Sam to find a way to survive on his own. With no work experience, no marketable skills, and no future, what was Sam to do?

Freefare came along just in time. Sam enrolled immediately and just like Joe received everything he needed to survive. Unlike Joe, Sam's first call came from the Freefare Drug Counseling Center. They were well aware of Sam's history of using drugs. They informed Sam of the requirement to attend mandatory drug counseling to remain in the program. In his first drug counseling program, he was given the option of checking in to the free drug campus. Sam elected not to go. After a number of sessions, Sam discontinued his use of drugs and was allowed to rent an apartment in nearby Hamburg, New York. Suddenly he is Joe Smith's next-door neighbor.

Just like Joe, Sam's next call came from the Freefare Food and Clothing Control Board. Sam had also started the program by purchasing nutritionally poor food groups. Sam was subjected to exactly the same process as Joe. Adherence to the nutrition process became much easier when Joe and Sam began to plan and prepare nutritionally sound meals together. They shared the meal preparation duties and found that with peer support the new diet was much more tolerable.

The Freefare Medical Control Board then sent a staff advisor to explain the health insurance coverage benefits and to assist in the implementation of a comprehensive wellness plan. The wellness program required Joe and Sam to regularly log on to the Freefare wellness website and enter their specific activities completed to achieve compliance with their individually designed wellness plan. Any failure to comply with the wellness program would trigger a follow-up visit. Failure to comply after the follow-up visit would lead to the loss of entertainment dollars on the entertainment debit card.

Next came a visit from a representative from the Freefare Entertainment Control Board. The representative met with each of them separately to explain the limitations applicable to the entertainment debit card. The representative showed them how to achieve additional benefits by adhering to their nutrition and wellness plans. They were also advised that the entertainment benefits could be restricted should they fail to comply with any Freefare control plans.

Both Joe and Sam were given all they needed to survive without any obligation to seek employment or live in a rundown tenement. Consider, if you will, what may have occurred had Freefare not been available. Joe was on the verge of engaging in a criminal life, and Sam was already dealing pot. Both could easily have evolved into hardened criminals. Instead, both found a safe and happy environment where they spent their time playing video games on their big-screen TV and surfing the Internet. Sam no longer smokes pot, as he has no means to purchase the drug. Joe is considering enrolling in a local college using the tuition-paid Freefare fund. Freefare removed both as a threat to society. No welfare, no jail time, no court costs, no violence. What's that worth?

When Freefare was first passed, Wanda lived with her six kids in a subsidized housing complex in a rundown area of Cleveland, Ohio. Wanda was a single parent working two jobs to fund her survival and finance day care for the children. The kids had been fathered by three different men, none of whom remained with Wanda. Only one of the fathers paid child support, and even he only made a meager contribution for the children. Wendy, Wanda's thirteen-year-old daughter, served as a surrogate mother to her siblings while Wanda worked long hours at two jobs. The ability to control and properly supervise five siblings ranging in age from six to twelve was becoming impossible for Wendy. Problems were occurring at school, and the police had been to the apartment several times. Child and Family Services was in the process of building a case to place the kids in foster care. The prospect for the kids was dim.

Freefare arrived just in time. Wanda enrolled immediately. She quit both her jobs and relished the opportunity to stay home and look after the kids. She obtained a new apartment in a quality neighborhood, bought new wardrobes, welcomed the nutrition counselors, and scheduled wellness visits for the kids with their new pediatrician. The children were given specialized psychological counseling and were immediately enrolled in a new school in a well-established middle-class neighborhood. With a new car, a full tank of gas, new clothes for everyone, a nutritionally sound diet supported by regular visits from the nutrition coach (both on-line and in-person), dental care, and a stay-at-home mother, life for Wanda and her children changed for the better. Six kids exposed to a dangerous environment were "rescued" and introduced to a whole new world! What would they have become without Freefare? How many of Wanda's six children would repeat her cycle of life and find themselves in the same situation she was in? Programs that currently exist would have effected little change in their environment. Food stamps, rental assistance, school-sponsored meal programs, and day care subsidies would have had very little impact on the overall environment in which they were living. They would have continued to be poor, living in a slum, interacting with peers surviving in the same environment. Without Freefare, it is a good bet that all of them would be unproductive members of society. Is the cost of saving them worth it?

Bill and Sue were recent retirees living in rural Western Pennsylvania. Both had steady work throughout their careers. However, they earned only enough to fund their lifestyle. Neither put aside funds for their retirement. They believed social security and Medicare would be sufficient support for their retirement years. Soon after retirement, they began to suffer a number of repair problems with their house. They remortgaged to obtain the funds to complete all the repairs. A short time later, their ten-year-old auto began to experience mechanical problems. Eventually the vehicle was deemed beyond repair. The payment for the updated mortgage was already eating up all their free cash. Another payment for a replacement vehicle was out of the question. The heating bill was skyrocketing due to a harsh winter. They were forced to make partial payments for their utilities so they could buy groceries. Depressed and desperate, they made the decision to enroll in Freefare. They signed the house over to the Freefare system, closed the checking account, and packed everything they owned for a move to a nearby apartment. Concerned at first at becoming wards of the state, they soon were relieved and unstressed.

Grateful for their relief, both soon became active volunteers to support causes benefiting their community. Freefare saved them, and they were determined to give back. Both began to volunteer in community programs to aid the handicapped. They also served as transition counselors for senior citizens making the decision to enroll in the Freefare program. Their personal experience made them perfect advisors to all who resisted the transition. Most of the seniors they counseled were facing significant financial challenges but had resisted enrollment into the Freefare system because they were raised to be self-supporting and had been productive citizens all their lives (as were Bill and Sue). Bill and Sue had faced the same issues and soon embraced the understanding that the Freefare program was developed as a replacement for social security and Medicare, programs that all workers contributed to throughout their entire working careers. Bill and Sue's reassurances made the transition to Freefare much easier for the retirees they were working with. Bill and Sue were active advocates of Freefare for the balance of their lives. When they passed away, all funeral expenses were paid by Freefare. There was no estate left behind, but Bill and Sue lived far richer lives than they would have on their own.

Ray and Beth were married with two children, a boy age nine and a girl age six. Ray was a successful sales representative for a national grocery chain. Beth was a stay-at-home mom, electing to be there for the kids as Ray was frequently away on business. They lived in an affluent neighborhood near Cincinnati, Ohio. Suddenly, without warning, their financial situation deteriorated. Beth noticed a significant decrease in their savings, and Ray was withdrawing sizable amounts of cash from the checking account. When Beth questioned Ray, he told her he was making an investment in something he could not reveal to anyone until it was time. Ray seemed increasingly stressed and was spending all his free time pursuing his new investment. The substance of the new investment came to light late one night when Beth received a call from the Cincinnati police. Ray had been found unconscious in a local motel. He had been rushed to the hospital and was in critical condition, apparently from an overdose of cocaine. Fortunately Ray survived and was able to recover within a few days. Ray then informed Beth that he had been addicted for several months and the addiction had affected his performance at work. He had missed several important meetings, causing his employer to fire him. The firing had been the trigger for the overdose. Ray informed Beth that he was moving to the newly established Freefare drug campus were he could continue to pursue his addiction for free.

Beth, jobless and untrained for a suitable job, was suddenly left on her own to figure things out. Drained of cash, with little or no equity in their house and two young children to raise, she was in desperate straits. After examining her options, Beth elected to enroll in Freefare. The house, vehicles, checking and savings accounts were turned over to the system. Beth and the kids packed their belongings and moved into a nearby apartment. Beth embraced all of the assistance programs offered in the Freefare program. Her children would benefit from the nutrition counseling, and they would all receive comprehensive medical care and wellness counseling. She viewed the Freefare control boards as an effective support system to help raise her family. Freefare saved them from a life of desperation and hardship!

These stories and thousands like them occur every day in America. In the past, a system bogged down in bureaucracy with tons of red tape and meager benefits would have condemned everyone cited above to a life of misery and suffering. Relegated to the bottom rung of the economic ladder, they would have barely survived, and the future for the children involved would have been hopeless. Freefare saved them all.

Now let's consider how Freefare will affect the composition of American cities. The escalating demand for apartments in appealing neighborhoods will create a tremendous opportunity for developers to create residential development zones that effectively integrate private homes with multiunit apartment buildings. In every city, slums will be leveled and replaced by new residential zones integrated with retail, entertainment, and grocery outlets, all readily available to the new residents. These privately owned business enterprises will be strongly supported by the Freefare debit card holders. Walk in health care facilities, wellness and nutrition centers, pharmacies, and fitness clubs will be integrated within walking distance for most residents. Auto sales and auto service centers will be popping up everywhere to sell and service the new fleet of Freefare automobiles. Inner-city real estate will suddenly become a valuable commodity. The construction industry will experience an economic boom not seen since the 1950s. Retailers and grocers will be scrambling to secure their spots in the new integrated communities. The job market will explode, and the average daily wage will skyrocket as the demand for new jobs will greatly outpace the supply of available labor (Freefare had removed a significant percentage of the potential job candidates that may have been previously available). Total transformation!

Everyone in America will be living in a safe environment, eating nutritious meals, fully insured for medical and dental care, and completely secure, knowing that Freefare will be the safety net to catch them should disaster strike. Crime rates will drop dramatically as slums transform into new residential zones and the drug users migrate to the free drug campuses. All barriers to quality education will be eliminated. Everyone will attend first-rate elementary and high schools, many of them newly constructed in the residential zones that replaced the slum areas. Freefare graduates will be given total access to any college they choose at no out-of-pocket cost and with no student loans.

All of these benefits are within our grasp. Sufficient funding will become available as soon as the majority of American voters concede authority to the federal establishment to eliminate the current tax codes and replace them with an honest redefinition of what our taxes actually are, a peaceful wealth redistribution system. Political leadership will become authorized to determine what levels of income (both personal and business) are fair to the new society. They will then use their new wealth redistribution authority to redirect the excess income directly to the Freefare program. The extent of funding needed to support Freefare will determine the amount of redistribution required. Personal and business income caps will be determined by the amount of financing needed. The size of the population supported within the Freefare program will become the key element used to determine the appropriate level for the income caps. The greater the number of Freefare participants, the lower the level of maximum income. The new federal system will seize the excesses and properly redistribute them directly to the Freefare program.

Consider the income of many professional athletes. Joe the baseball player signs a new contract that pays him $10 million per year. The new wealth redistribution system establishes a fair personal income cap at an annual income level of $2 million. The players' $8 million in excess earnings becoming fully taxed and directed the Freefare system. The income cap would quickly force the professional athlete and their agents to adjust their contract demands likely negotiating lifetime annuity agreements that would allow the player to receive an annual income for the remainder of his or her life. Diminishing annual player contract expenses would drive up team profits. Freefare earnings caps would also apply to the team income forcing team owners to manage the excesses (likely by lowering prices) as the Freefare system will capture all excess wealth earned by the team.

The successful main-street business owner will face a similar situation. The $2 million income cap will limit the personal income he can earn from the business. If he elects to take exactly $2 million, the business will then likely exceed the fair business income level and the funds he failed to take for himself will still be subject to redistribution based upon the maximum wealth level set for the business. As an alternative, the business could manage excess profit by increasing the wages of employees, paying employees greater benefits, or lowering prices. All adjustments would benefit society.

The Freefare system, functioning properly, will effectively diminish the number of Freefare participants over time and thereby increase the future cap on personal and business income. The improved living conditions, community influences, and advanced education opportunities will serve to develop useful citizens capable of securing meaningful employment and thus exiting the Freefare program. It is probable that the initial older Freefare participants will remain in the system for an extensive period. However, their children and the younger initial participants will likely become much more self-reliant and quickly opt out of the system. Businesses and wealthy individuals will be motivated to assist participants in exiting the Freefare system as the wealth redistribution income caps will be a direct function of how much of the population is enrolled in Freefare. Despite the enriched environment, there will always be a segment of the population that either cannot or will not work. Therefore, the Freefare program will become a permanent part of our future.

The ultimate appeal of the Freefare program to our political leaders is the degree of control that can be exerted over the program participants. Every activity undertaken by the Freefare participants will be monitored, analyzed, and controlled. Behavior deemed to be inappropriate will lead to immediate intervention from one or more of the control boards assigned to manage the affected behavior. All economic activity will involve the use of a specific debit card that is monitored on a 24-7 basis. The use of cash by Freefare participants will be outlawed, assuring that every financial transaction can be continually tracked and evaluated. Control board intervention will be activated as soon as any significant behavioral deviation is detected. The entire group will be monitored, managed, and controlled by the various control boards that oversee the use of the debit cards. Everything from the size of soda drinks, the type of clothing, the degree of fast food, wellness compliance, alcohol consumption, doctor visits, dental care, and hundreds of other categories will be set up for intervention should the participant deviate from the control board standards. Enforcing compliance will be relatively easy, considering the participant will be totally dependent upon the availability of funds on the debit card to purchase anything. Limiting the funds available or even turning off a debit card will arm the control board with sufficient means to properly motivate those who are not in compliance with board standards. Freefare participants will quickly become complacently compliant to the standards set by their control board overseers, totally removing them as any type of threat to society.

The economic benefits of the program will eliminate poverty. No longer will there exist an underprivileged class that threatens the tranquility of our society. Wealth envy will no longer be the prime motivation for political uprisings, as those without jobs will be fully provided for. Burglaries and robberies will become a thing of the past. As soon as Freefare is established and the free drug use campuses are opened, all motivation to commit these crimes will be eliminated. Political uprisings will also become a thing of the past. People who live in quality neighborhoods who are well fed, adequately dressed, and medically cared for will have little motivation to revolt!

Those citizens not participating in the Freefare program will be working and living in a safer environment. Over time, everyone (especially those who graduate from the Freefare program) will be healthier, better educated, and more productive. White-collar crime will likely continue, but the law enforcement operations investigating these crimes will not be bogged down (as they are now) dealing with drug dealers, break-ins, robberies, and other similar crimes commonly associated with economically challenged classes. Law enforcement will be transformed into an economic transaction enforcement unit trained to focus on white-collar crimes. Well-armed SWAT units will no longer be needed.

Freefare will become the twenty-first century's means to control all governed constituencies. No longer will armed combat be the preferred path to conquest and control. Fear and repression will be replaced by this new peaceful means to control the population. Power across the globe will be seized by those politicians who promise a peaceful, nondestructive, fairer system of wealth distribution, Freefare. These politicians will be brought to power based upon their ability to properly institute and manage fair caps on business and personal income. Earning limits will be set to achieve sufficient cash flows to fund Freefare. The primary domestic function of future governments will be the proper management of wealth redistribution levels. Twenty-first-century politicians will be fully authorized to determine how much wealth is enough. Then leveraging the consent of the governed, they will use their political authority to seize whatever earnings they determine to be excess and redirect it to those who are unwilling or unable to properly support themselves. Freefare will become not only the means to financially provide for those in need, but it will also provide the control mechanism to properly manage the lives of those receiving the benefits.

Freefare will be an easy sell to our control-hungry federal guardians. The only holdback will be their perception of their capability to redirect sufficient funds to finance the program. Will they successfully find consensus to terminate ineffective traditional programs that are managed by a bloated bureaucracy full of political appointees, or will they continue to add redundant counterproductive programs? The well-established wealth redistribution aspects of our current tax laws provide the means to obtain the funds needed to finance Freefare. If our federal legislators can stop squandering the funds they Robin Hood from successful Americans and properly deploy the funds to truly help the needy, objections to paying a fair share will quickly diminish.

Instituting Freefare will require a champion to lead the movement, someone capable of simulating the first hundred days of Franklin Roosevelt's New Deal. Full transition will require a similar revolutionary aspect—out with the old and in with the new. Once those in need grasp the extent of the potential benefits, there will be no stopping their demand to institute the program, and every political leader will forced to jump on board and support the program.

A significant number of challenges must be met once the Freefare program is adopted; enrollment platforms, debit card issuance, locating and constructing appropriate housing, control board staffing, vehicle availability, adequate food supplies, adequate clothing supplies, termination of all existing traditional welfare programs, and health insurance enrollment. Removing older Freefare participants from the social security program will be among the most critical. Successfully accomplishing all of this will indeed be a challenge, but it can be done!

Think of how it will transform America: apartment construction will boom, slums will be leveled and replaced with new integrated communities, demand for new automobiles will soar, demand for nutritional food supplies will skyrocket, and job growth will be unprecedented, accompanied by an increasing average wage growth as labor supply will be limited by those who opt for Freefare and drop out of the labor market. A rebirth of the American dream. The Utopian society achieved! No one homeless, no one hungry, crime rates at unheard-of lows, full employment at livable wages, and a functioning safety net for anyone faced with financial catastrophe.

Freefare is the answer!

AFTERWORD

Presidents Wilson, Roosevelt, and Johnson based their presidential agendas on the belief that America's free-enterprise economic system had failed a significant segment of the population. All three believed that it was the duty of all who were benefiting from the free-enterprise system to subsidize those whom the system had failed.

FDR, the most impactful of the three, totally transformed the role of the federal government when he accepted federal responsibility to protect the common man from the consequences of the free-enterprise system's failure to include everyone in the wealth distribution opportunity. His New Deal permanently injected federal participation into virtually every working American's paycheck and added substantial federal control over nearly every aspect of the American economy (social security, minimum-wage laws, farm subsidies, fair labor practices laws). Once he successfully established his New Deal, the role of the president would be forever married to the expectation the president would champion relief to any class of society economically suffering in America.

In the 1960s, Lyndon Johnson doubled down on the New Deal by establishing his own version of social responsibility, the Great Society. It served to permanently

153

establish the expectation of federal intervention to correct any imperfections (real or perceived) in American wealth distribution process. After LBJ's term ended, people in America embraced the concept that being American entitled them to a meaningful standard of existence regardless of the circumstances that caused their conditions.

In the hundred years that have passed since Woodrow Wilson first introduced the income tax, America evolved from a land of opportunity into a land of social responsibility. Freefare is, very logically, the next phase in America's utopian journey. No one can argue against the benefits Freefare represents. No American needs to suffer economic depravity, there will be no homeless families, and no child will go to bed hungry. The social engineering aspects of the program (proper nutrition, integrated housing, free college education) will provide a meaningful pathway for the next generation to become hardworking, productive, well-nourished citizens. No more "I had to escape the hood," no more "I had to join a gang to survive." Every citizen will be properly fed, housed in a respectable neighborhood, and encouraged to pursue higher education.

America's final entry into the Freefare entitlement world is only one small step away. We will fully enter the age of entitlement once the voting majority confirms that everything any individual needs to thrive in America is a fundamental right.

Only through the establishment of Freefare can America activate all the elements required to fulfill that promise and endow these perceived rights on anyone existing on American soil.

The concept of Freefare will not only eliminate poverty but also provide every recipient a pathway to escape the economic conditions that have for centuries suppressed millions of potentially productive citizens. Americans simply need to acknowledge the advent of the age of entitlement. It's a step that requires everyone to embrace a new, updated version of the American dream—exchanging the founding fathers' concept of total freedom for a new, fully managed, socially responsible society.

Printed in the United States
by Baker & Taylor Publisher Services